OUT OF THE
FAR EAST

BY
ALLAN A. HUNTER

FRIENDSHIP PRESS

NEW YORK

Reprinted in 1972 by R and E Research
Associates, publishers and distributors of
ethnic studies. 4843 Mission Street, San
Francisco, California 94112 and 18581 Mc
Farland Avenue, Saratoga, California 95070
Editor: Adam S. Eterovich
Publisher: Robert D. Reed

Library of Congress
Card Catalog No.

78-155192

ISBN 0-88247-193-7

To
ELIZABETH

ALLAN A. HUNTER was born in Canada and passed his early boyhood there and in Denver, Colorado. He went to high school in Riverside, California, and attended Occidental College for a year. He took his bachelor's degree from Princeton University in 1916 and then taught for two years in Egypt on the staff of Assiut College. In the summer of 1917 he served three months with the Y.M.C.A. among Allenby's troops in the Sinai Desert campaign. In 1918 he joined the American Red Cross unit in Palestine and later served with Near East Relief as deputy director of the Syrian Orphanage in Jerusalem.

In 1920 Mr. Hunter returned to America by way of India and the Far East where he spent several months studying social and political conditions. For the following four years he was a student at Union Theological Seminary, New York City, and also did graduate work in education at Teachers College, Columbia University, where he took his M.A. degree in 1925. In 1923 he was married to Miss Elizabeth Walker of Los Angeles.

In the autumn of 1925 Mr. and Mrs. Hunter went to the Far East under the Fellowship of Youth for Peace and spent a year in university centers of China and Japan teaching and developing friendly contacts between the youth of the Orient and the United States. Since returning to America Mr. Hunter has been minister of the Mount Hollywood Community (Congregational) Church, Los Angeles.

In his ministry and in his close association with many student and youth groups both on the Pacific Coast and in other parts of the United States, Mr. Hunter has formed a wide acquaintance among young people of Oriental origin and has made a special study of their problems.

CONTENTS

CHAPTER ONE

OUT OF THE FAR EAST

IT IS the last lap for the leaders in the five thousand meter race of the Tenth International Olympic, which is being held, for the first time in its history, in the United States. Fifty thousand excited spectators rise from their seats at the Los Angeles Coliseum. They strain their necks, some of them clench their fists as if they themselves were pushing the last ounce of energy into this struggle. Tense with excitement, almost breathless with suspense and releasing its pent-up emotions with hoarse cries, that huge crowd almost shares the agony of the struggling contestants.

Then a ripple of admiration passes over those thousands. For one of the runners, a short, bow-legged Japanese, although a whole lap behind the Finn and the American who are up ahead, does a sportsmanlike thing that takes the breath away. Obviously he is utterly exhausted. Nevertheless he moves over to the right and motions to the man trying to pass him to take the inside lane. The same courtesy he shows to every succeeding runner that overtakes him.

The Finn is ahead. His legs flash in the California afternoon sun with the almost perfect rhythm of a machine. How strangely effortless appears that clean-cut body speeding around the last bend! But you know from the perspiration running down your own brow and the tenseness of your own clenched fists and straining neck that every fiber of muscle, every drop of blood, every resource of will, is being subordinated and bent to one supreme effort, not to quit but to keep on going. The American, with longer legs and broader shoulders, has been creeping up on the Finn at an implacable pace. The head wobbles just enough to betray the agony of his fatigue. See! he is swerving to the right. He is trying to pass.

But the man in front moves over and stays in the way. The American now heads for the inside lane. But the Finn, possibly anticipating this move, now seems to be swinging back to the left, thus cutting across the path of his rival. Deliberately? Who knows? Anyone who has himself run "long distance" and listened for ten minutes to that last nerve-racking debate in his solar plexus, "Now I'll quit—no, I won't; now I'll quit—no, I won't," can sympathize with the Finn for that apparent misstep in sportsmanship which shocks the crowd. If only his coach had ingrained into him not only the determination to win at all costs but the spirit that refuses to block another man! In any event, what those men are showing is a miracle of disciplined courage.

Just look at that! Neck to neck now. What a spurt! Who broke the tape first? Who won? That must be a new world record. You'd think they'd drop in a heap after a race like that. But there they are standing at the side of the cinder track and watching the others come in. The crowd is still roaring.

But soon attention shifts to a bobbing head wearing a white cap, apparently to keep the sweat out of his eyes. His legs must be only half as long as the American champion's, but they are a shade browner. He's that little Japanese chap who couldn't keep up with this fast company but who insisted on being so amazingly, so orientally polite. After he finishes this lap he's got another one to go. But surely he'll quit. No, sir. He isn't going to give in, not Takenaka. Look at him pounding away there. You can tell by his wobbling head that he's all in—absolutely all in. I'll bet he can't see anything at all except the general direction ahead. I wonder if he can hear the crowd yelling for him. Come on, Japan, come on! You've got the stuff! All the other runners are spectators now. The Nipponese is the only one left on the track.

The crowd rises again. As he takes the turn, swaying now like a drunken man, and levels out for the last awful stretch to where he vaguely knows there is an end to this torture in stomach and legs and arms, a great murmur of admiration goes out for this lonely runner from the Far East, and then, as he collapses in a faint beyond the finish, a prolonged cheer.

There is more enthusiasm in that cheer than the winners received—more even than the American was awarded earlier in the afternoon when he established a new four hundred meter world record. Perhaps no man in the entire Olympic is to get such a whole-hearted ovation as this.

That lone runner returns to the Far East. But what of those out of the Far East who live within our shores? There are more than a quarter of a million Orientals in the United States, not including Hawaii. They are guests or fellow-citizens of this country. Look again at that game, slant-eyed athlete who is representative of them. He is a symbol of their concentrated effort. With us they are participating in an event requiring the utmost of endurance, muscle and skill. But in this case the prize is not a wreath of olive leaves. Figuratively, the struggle is just as desperate, the competition just as keen, when it is the less spectacular business of living and making a living.

Here they are, nearly 140,000 Japanese, about 75,000 Chinese, somewhat fewer than 50,000 Filipinos, a thousand or so Koreans, and perhaps 3,000 Hindus; guests or fellow citizens. And, when you stop to think, it is a mighty gallant fight they are putting up against stiff odds. We find them scattered across the land, more in the Far West than in the East, on farms, in Little Tokyos, in Chinatowns, in transient fruit-picking communities. Some of them blur past us as we stare through the railway window, vague, stooped figures that never seem to tire of picking berries and cutting asparagus. Others we glance at curiously through the open door of a small laundry. A few we notice in chop suey restaurants and curio stores. Still others we pass on the campus hurrying to lectures, a pile of books under the arm; these foreign students seem to be more anxious to get there than we are. The straight black hair, almond eyes, high cheek bones, tan or olive skins, these of course are only masks. It may be that behind those masks we can discover what sometimes we sense within ourselves, a secret feeling of inadequacy, a desire to overcome obstacles, and—who knows?—the same Olympic passion for perfection.

Take that erect well-groomed Filipino who has just stepped out of the Chicago Art Museum. You call to him. He does not at first notice. When, out of breath, you overtake him on the sidewalk waiting for the "Go" signal, he is surprised. It is a little embarrassing. Then you explain that you simply want to chat with him, if he can spare a few minutes, because you want to get the point of view of a Filipino like himself. At first he is evidently suspicious, resentful. You mention that you know Dr. Frank Laubach out in Manila, the man who has recently been translating American jokes into the language of the Moros and teaching them to read in several lessons. A common friend; the ice is broken. "Now tell me," you urge perhaps too eagerly, "how do you feel about being here, now that you've been in this country more than four years?"

He hesitates; you urge him to go ahead. And he does:

"Well, it takes the self-confidence out of most of us. I work in that hotel over there five hours a day and study at night. It isn't the strenuous hours; I don't mind hard work. It's the contempt that everybody seems to have for me. They think I'm a cook or a washerman or what they call a 'boy.' It would be easy for me to look down on myself, what with these pin-pricks every day, and everybody acting as if a fellow with my skin couldn't really amount to anything. I was cynical for quite a while, like most of my friends. But I'm just about out of that stage now. Come on over to our club. We'll have a chat alone and I'll tell you my story."

The club proves to be the Filipino Community Center maintained under Christian auspices. Outside are a dozen fine-looking fellows talking with a great deal of animation, presumably about the bill that would give independence to the Filipinos on condition that Uncle Sam may export what he likes into the Islands, without duty, while at the same time he raises a tariff wall against Filipino imports. You invite your new acquaintance to have a cup of coffee in the little restaurant in the basement of this dormitory.

"What did you eat when you were a boy over in the Islands?" is your opening to conversation. The question is like a match lighting up hidden memories. Within a few minutes the scenes described are so real and vivid that it is as if you are Juan himself tying up the water buffalo for the night and then coming for supper to the little cottage. Before a table a foot and a half high you sit on the bamboo floor under the thatched roof with father and mother and brothers and sisters, and fall to. There is pot roast of pork with perhaps a mudfish caught that morning in the river beyond the mango trees; a salad of bamboo shoots, onions and tomatoes; some unpolished rice; and pineapple picked that afternoon. . . .

You are especially hungry this night, for all day you have been trying to persuade the water buffalo to pull the old wooden plough a little faster, and wood had to be brought in for the evening cooking. Besides, it won't be long now before there will be no more suppers like this, for you're headed for the high seas, and America is your goal. The father sees little sense in a seventeen-year-old boy going off on a fool's adventure; isn't Juan just beginning to show that he can make a success of cabbages and beans and squash? However, he will help you borrow enough pesos to get that steamship ticket. . . .

How marvelous America will be! Skyscrapers (maybe I'll be owning one when I come back and show my pockets bulging with gold). Education (think how I'll be looked up to as senator of this province). Experience (why, America has the greatest mines, the greatest stockyards, the greatest railroads in the world . . . George Washington, Abraham Lincoln. . . . America's the land where everybody can have "life, liberty and the pursuit of happiness"; that's what we learned in school, and it's what the American teacher is always telling us). And success (look at Sylvestre! The steamship agent says that after he returned from San Francisco he became director of public health for the province. Look at Gregorio, he was just four years over there, but doesn't he practically own the whole town now? "You can do it too, if you have the courage, young man, the ambition"). . . .

The thirty-day trip in the steerage is not quite up to the steamship agent's glowing description. Your fellow passengers make fun of your pants that fit so tight and they call you a "hick." No one ever suggested that seasickness was as bad as this. You clench your fists and say to yourself, "I wish I hadn't come, but I won't be a quitter." Eventually you see the Golden Gate and the tawny hills of California, not the vivid green of those back home, but solid land.

Leaving the pier for a thronging street you can hardly realize that your dream is fulfilled. You smile uncontrollably. America! America! The land I've longed to see is here now . . . "Hello, hello, hello," you feel like crying to everybody passing by. You march up to the traffic cop. "Where is the Filipino club?"

"What?" he asks incredulously.

Thinking him deaf you present your card. He pays no attention. You stop a woman crossing the street and in your most courteous manner say, "Madam, can you direct me to the Filipino club?" She imagines she is being accosted and gets excited: "I'll have you arrested."

Then—you're only seventeen—you set your wicker suitcase down on the curb and burst into tears. A stranger noticing you so depressed comes up: "Say, Filipino, are you from Alongupo (the naval station in the Philippines)? Do you know the Mandino dance hall?" But he doesn't take the time to show you how to get to your destination. Another man addresses you. "Come with me to the International Hotel." When you get there, you begin to sense something wrong. A fellow Filipino takes you aside and tells you how you have a chance to meet worthwhile girls here that you would never meet in the Islands. Just then an American,—whom you later get to know as the missionary who always makes it a point to watch for newly-arrived Filipinos and offer them help,—takes you into confidence. "This is no place for you. I'll take you to Berkeley." . . .

Later, in the college town, a Filipino student breaks you in, and shows you how to cook and wait on table. The woman for whom he is working allows you to share his room and board. Before long you have the job and your employer helps you to enter the high school. The teachers are sympathetic and they do what they can. You get along well with the fellows because you play tolerably good baseball and basketball. But you are never invited into a home for any social gathering. An older Filipino, with whom you compare notes, gives his experience: at another university he walked across the campus with a white girl and some of the fellows threw cigarettes at him. Once, however, a high school junior asks you to have an ice cream with him. He is a poor boy and you are surprised. But his motive is somewhat mixed. "Tell me," he asks, "about the Philippines. What chance has an American fellow to make a little money out there?" . . .

Then comes the Depression. You are let off because the household expenses must be cut down. But Watsonville, where there ought to be work in the lettuce fields, is only about one hundred miles distant. You start out to walk. When you were a youngster you set off alone for high school over the hills fifty miles away. . . .

This lettuce country isn't what you had expected. For more than eight hours a day you stoop over, hoeing and then cutting lettuce heads under a sun that makes you wish you had your two-foot Filipino straw hat. At night you find yourself herded with a gang of tired men into a barn with bunks, and no insect powder available. One of the men who knows the ropes advises you never, under any circumstances, to be seen walking with a white girl; it's too dangerous. "Just forget that dream you had of this country, equality in work and play. Above all, keep away from American girls entirely. Watch your step. The law won't allow you anything that looks like a dirk; you carry a knife all the same. These white men are liable to do anything to you. If they strip off your clothes and send you off without a stitch, that's getting off easy." . . .

But, after three months of bending over the lettuce, row on endless row, with no one interesting to talk to, no fun, just homesickness and the first exhilaration all gone, you decide one warm evening after your supper of boiled rice that you can't stand being bored any longer; so you drift over to the hall not far from the town where there will be music and dancing and a chance to forget the crude talk of the men.

Some white men used to run this roadhouse, but recently it has been rented by Filipinos who have hired a dozen or so American girls to dance with the lettuce workers. You pay your money at the door and sit down timidly to watch the fellows from the camp having a good time; you don't have the courage yet to ask one of those girls to show you these new steps. What was the use of coming any way? Why not go back to the bunk house?

Suddenly a strange look comes over the faces of some of the dancers. That noise outside, what is it? Something's up out there. You rush out and face a mob of angry men and boys shaking their fists and shouting curses at you. They grab you and search through your clothes, but find no weapon in your pockets, fortunately. A big American slaps your face with his left hand and with his right points a revolver at your stomach. "Get out or we'll kill you!" You run for it. A few seconds later shots ring out, evidently not aimed at you. . . .

You head towards Los Angeles, three hundred and fifty miles south. There you hear that an automobile full of rowdies emptied their guns into your camp at

Watsonville and a bullet pierced the heart of one of the fellows as he slept in his bunk. He was a quiet chap, but he was always ready to listen to your troubles. If only Tobera had been less serious and had gone with you to the dance, he might now be enjoying the sight of the California hills turning green under the sunshine.

You hear also that most of the white people in this city named after the angels are down on you and your countrymen. You deposit a fee of five dollars in an employment bureau, but the job which they get for you, the job of "bus boy," carrying dishes in a hotel, lasts just one week. The bureau, of course, keeps the fee, and doesn't make any effort to get you another job. Later you check with other Filipinos to discover that this is the usual way the employment bureaus work with the inexperienced. . . .

But this is not the only racket that takes you in. The taxi dance hall empties your pockets—one dime a dance —and the Chinese gambling houses, where there is free rice and music, get the rest of your money. In time you find yourself standing around the tables as close as you can to any Filipino that seems to be winning in the hope that he will give you a nickel. Sometimes you fool the cop and sleep in the park, but generally you spend the night, hungry and dilapidated, with nine or ten other men in the room of a friend. Your fellow countrymen have lost a good deal since coming to America; but the capacity of Filipinos to share, they have not let that go.

Bitter, you say to yourself: America is not what I was told. The Americans are a bunch of hypocrites, exploiters. Altruism? There's no such thing in all this country. I'm going back to tell the Filipinos what a country this is and what the people are really like. They are not Christians. We are better Christians than they are. Here we've been fooled all these years. I'll work for a revolution to drive the Americans out of our country. You even repeat to a friend what you heard an orator shout, "We Filipinos should unite behind the banner of Nippon for the salvation of Asia from the tyranny and oppression of the white races. . . . Every American dollar invested in the Philippines is one more nail in the coffin of Philippine independence." . . .

Once, on a Sunday evening, you climb the stone steps of a great new church on the boulevard. An important looking man, at the top, greets you and whispers hastily, "This is not for your race."

Now the interesting thing is that no matter how low you get, nor how much self-pity you indulge in, you never seriously think of going communist or taking your life. That is because it is ingrained in you to believe in the sanctity of the home and in Bathala, the

Super-Spirit that always keeps watch over you no matter what is happening; suicide would mean you would not be acceptable to him or join him after you died.

You hear that the feeling against Filipinos is not so strong farther East. You join a party of Filipinos Chicago-bound in an old Ford. . . .

In the city there are odd jobs you find to do, but you are still confused, bewildered; you cannot see that you are getting anywhere. One night a stranger, from a province near yours back in the Islands, asks you to his room. Something in his face warms you. You would like to have that quality yourself. He tells you how he went around in a blind eddy for two years after arriving here, but one day an American invited him to spend an evening with him in his home. In front of an open fire after supper what that host did seemed to throw light on something new in America; an American could understand your situation; an American could treat you as a human being.

Your new friend invites you to the home of this unusual American who, you later hear, helped to organize the Community Center and who actually does practise what so many talk about. Before long you are in the same Christian fellowship with your Filipino friend, and as you talk things over and make plans together with this group, you feel again that life does have meaning after all.

If the Filipino, whose experiences we have just been sharing, is sometimes confused as he gropes his way into the complexities of the big city, how about the Japanese who is born here, who salutes the flag not as subject but as citizen, who has the same tastes and ambitions as those of fairer skins calling themselves Americans? Consider Mary Yamamoto, attractive, well-groomed, alert.

The other night, at a young people's meeting, a blonde high school senior recalled how a couple of years previously she had attended a girls' conference at which a Japanese was elected "mayor." Five or six of the delegates had withdrawn because they did not wish to have an Oriental over them. Their act had been approved by one of the young people in the meeting, but heavily criticized by others, who protested, "Why shouldn't she be mayor? She is an American citizen. And, anyway, this is a Christian conference." Well, at this meeting, after the senior's story of race prejudice had been heard, the group asked the leader to locate a Japanese undergraduate of the Junior College and bring her as a guest the following Sunday to discuss with the group her experiences and observations as a second-generation Japanese.

When the group leader called on Mary Yamamoto he found her living in a two-story house not in "Little Tokyo" but in one of the more conventional zones in the city from which Oriental residents are not barred. On the table were magazines printed in Japanese for the old folks; there was the regular morning paper, and also the *Japanese American News* and the *Japan California Daily News,* half in English, and half in Japanese. Over the mantel stood an exquisite cloisonné bowl. The pictures on the walls included a Hofmann. Mary introduced her mother, who bowed charmingly with a touch of the old-fashioned Japanese courtesy. Her halting English was totally different from that of the daughter. Mary's father was in his office downtown, the younger sister was playing tennis, the older brother, a columnist in English who worked at night on the Japanese paper, was still in bed.

The incident of the "mayor's" election at the girls' conference was cited as the reason why the group had invited Mary to address them frankly on the interracial problem, from an Oriental's viewpoint. Mary Yamamoto laughed a little self-consciously, but maintained her poise: "It so happens that I was that Japanese 'mayor.' But I won't be timid about speaking out. I have learned that we Japanese who were born here have an obligation to make our American friends see what we see."

At the meeting of the young people's group Mary Yamamoto began her story by describing her sister Shiro, who was about to be graduated from high school. This sister was president of a social club. She had a host of American friends, and she was planning to enter the university that fall. "But I am going to forewarn her," said Mary, "those girls at the high school who are so chummy with her now will cut her on the college campus; not deliberately or consciously, of course. Just the same they will not be seen walking with a Japanese; that might queer their chances of making the sorority they want to get into. Can you see how we Japanese gradually learn to shelter ourselves by sticking to our own group so that we won't have our feelings hurt? If we become too intimate with an American girl, later on she may act as if we do not exist.

"I often try to imagine how you Americans feel towards people like me. Last month I read in a magazine [1] an editorial saying that we Japanese in California are all armed and ready to cut your throats as you sleep in bed. That editorial even suggested that we had instructions—those of us who are employed—to poison our American employers. Of course, I knew why the editor circulated all these silly rumors. He simply wanted to frighten you so you would be in favor of backing up a bigger navy; there had to be some sort of bogey-man. And I know that you have enough sense to see through that smoke screen and to

[1] See *Liberty*, March 25, 1933.

realize that we California-born Japanese are loyal citizens of this country. But do you really know us? Look at me. Outside—Japanese. And, if you take just my eyes and skin, I am an Oriental. But, inside, I am American. I go to beach parties. I like to dance and play tennis and read, sometimes the *Saturday Evening Post* and sometimes the *World Tomorrow*. If this were a Buddhist temple and not a Christian church, your guess as to what to do would be as good as mine. I do know some Japanese ideographs, but I'm not much good at talking the language. It's mighty awkward sometimes when I have to join in the general conversation at a gathering of older Japanese people. Every time I open my mouth I feel as if I'm making a *faux pas*.

"You would have laughed to see me the time I went over to Japan three years ago this summer. The Japanese over there sit on their ankles and the food is served on the floor. Well, when the soup was set before me my legs began to ache terribly, so I tried to change my position. And what do you think I did? I put my foot right into the soup. The maid in her bright pink kimono almost choked, she tried so hard not to laugh. At night there was no bed to sleep on, only a mat. Three times a day we had one or two bowls of rice, and sometimes raw fish with *shoyu* sauce, and tea all the time. Like any other American I would have swapped a day's rations for one cup of hot coffee and a slice of buttered toast.

"But when I was visiting my cousins in the Tokyo Girls' College the joke was on me. Just because I live in Hollywood they thought I should know all about 'Doug and Mary.' . . . It was certainly funny. They could tell me more than I knew about the movie stars of my home town. I didn't want to seem like a moron, and so I told them that once I had my hair cut by the barber who does it for Marlene Dietrich. So I did rate, after all. When they asked if there were any churches in Hollywood, any Sunday schools, I know for the first time how a Chinese must feel when you ask him about the bandits in Peiping, and whether the Chinese eat rats. It made me a little sore to discover how they thought about us here in Hollywood, as if we were barbarians, as if we spent most of our time watching for some screen hero to come out of a café, or trying to get in on wild parties. How would you like to be asked if there are any nice homes in the town you come from, and if it isn't true that just about everybody gets divorced? Well, some of our ideas about Japan and other nations are just about as silly as their ideas about Hollywood. Maybe you have notions about us second-generation Japanese that are just as unfair? Or romantic?

"Don't get the idea that we all can arrange flowers

beautifully and do the tea ceremony and practise jujutsu. There are one or two elderly ladies in Los Angeles
of the old samurai school who were trained in Japan
and who have the ancient traditions and tricks in their
blood. The other night a Los Angeles bandit held up
Madam Tsuta Hattori, seventy years old, and de-
manded her purse. Poor chap, before he knew what
had happened to him he had landed on his head in the
gutter. The old lady, proud of her samurai traditions,
had not forgotten her jujutsu.

"We American-born Japanese know practically
nothing of those ancient things. And, actually, we are
becoming different from the older generation even in
body, just as children of European immigrants differ
from their ancestral races in Europe. In Japan children
are carried on their mother's or older sister's back, and
you will find them quite bowlegged. Also, they squat
on their ankles, a custom which, by interfering with
the circulation of the blood, tends to shorten their legs.
But, as you know, my American-born generation sits
on chairs; we are generally bigger and stronger than
our parents, and certainly taller. I have friends whose
skin is so light they are sometimes mistaken for Spanish or Italian girls, and one girl passes for an American
when she wants to.

"The old folks are getting fewer and fewer. Last
year six thousand more Japanese left this country than

came into it. The birth rate of Japanese in America is
dropping; the average number of children in a Japanese family now is actually less than three. I don't
think you have to be afraid of the Japanese variety of
stork any more in the United States.

"But don't forget there are a lot of my group in this
country, about 73,000 in all, over against the 65,000
older Japanese who can never be citizens. In Los Angeles alone we number 8,000 (I have these figures because my sociology professor asked me to write a term
paper about it). Before long there will be in California 10,000 who will be eligible for voting. What
are you going to do about us?

"You may not let us into that select organization, the
Native Daughters of the Golden West. All the same
we pay our way here in California, and one of us,
Hiroshi Neeno, was elected president of the Roosevelt
High School student body the other day. We aren't
going to live in shacks without plumbing the way our
parents did, but we won't forget the service they ren-
dered to the West Coast, either. They took on jobs the
white people scorned, in the fields and on the railroads, and the whole West owes a lot to them. They
were the first to plant rice in California. They cultivated the fields from which come some of our best
celery, tomatoes and lettuce. By their labor they became just as much the pioneers of the old West as

the fathers and mothers of your Native Sons and Daughters of the Golden West.

"Later on, no doubt, we'll be there, but I challenge you to give one case of a Japanese to date standing in a breadline. As for crime, we have nothing as a racial group to be ashamed of.

"The trouble is that no matter how well trained we are, or how well we do at college, we can't find a place. I know it's hard enough for fellows and girls who have blue eyes and light hair to get a job these days. But it is three times as difficult for one of my American-born group because race prejudice puts in our path an extra high barrier.

"What occupations are there in which we are welcome? Yes, we can occasionally get work in a fruit stand or in a market or a florist's shop. But, suppose we wish to be doctors, teachers, dentists, lawyers, social workers, or ministers? Sometimes there is a chance in these fields. But we lack financial backing. After we go through the disappointment again and again of finding no opening, we wonder whether it is worth while, whether it isn't really a mistake for us to go to college. One makes no better living for having gone. In fact, the years at college are just lost. Why go, then? You end up by working in a fruit stand in any case. That's the way most of the young people, who are my friends, argue.

"To prepare my paper I went down to the produce market where our people sell their fruit and vegetables, and there I found fourteen college graduates. One of them was from California Tech. After graduation he got first place in the civil service examination, but because he was what they call a 'Jap' he was not acceptable in spite of his high marks. Now he loads a vegetable truck down there every night except Saturday from 7 P.M. to 7 A.M.

"Because of the attitude of white people towards us, we face not merely temporary difficulties due to the depression but a permanent handicap. I'm not complaining; I only want you to see the facts. Here we are, feeling like Americans and looking like foreigners, all dressed up and apparently no place to go."

Mary has stated the case of many second-generation Japanese. Let us put ourselves in the shoes of a Chinese here for only four years in an Eastern university. Jimmy Chen is not dressing himself up with vague or bitter expectations; he has a definite place to go. It won't be many months before he will be wielding important influence in that vast, exciting arena of conflicting forces called "China."

Jimmy had contact with this country long before he came over here. One day he and his playmates almost lost their kites, so amazed were they over some visitors marching through the village. The visitors were blue-eyed and yellow-haired, and they were from ships the color of thunder clouds that sometimes spoke like lightning. Those Americans were devils, foreign devils. When Jimmy studied at the mission school two hundred miles downstream he met a different kind of American, but he was still a little skeptical. They did not look so bad and they certainly were friendly. But how could one be sure they were not "running dogs of imperialism," plotting to hand China over to the foreign sailors and soldiers?

Within a few months after fixing up his room in the dormitory of a Philadelphia campus, Jimmy was so popular he had difficulty at times in getting his work done. At first his classmates would visit him out of curiosity; here was a scholar who could start in at dawn quoting from memory some of the old classics, stuff that he had learned as a youngster, and he could keep it up until sunset. Such, at least, was his reputation. And they soon found that Jimmy Chen had his own background. His ancestors were reciting Confucius when their own were running around in the forests of Britain sacrificing human beings and painting their own naked bodies with blue woad.

Before long Jimmy Chen was accepted everywhere, and a classmate invited him to dinner one night at "the house." A Western fraternity brother was at first a bit surprised to meet a "Chinaman" at the table, but managed to conceal his feelings. In the conversational free-for-all that followed around the fire, Jimmy had a great time enlightening the fellow from San Francisco. Why, no, he had never smoked opium. There was one province in China where the military government would order the farmers to grow poppies and later would collect fines from them for having broken the law; but where he lived the scourge of the soldiers and the bandits and the opium peddlers had never come. China, you see, was a big country. Yes, in some places parents still bound the feet of their daughters when they were five or seven years old, and you would sometimes hear them screaming at night; the tradition was that the ideal bride's feet were three inches long. But the government passed a law against all that, and Jimmy's sisters, one of them now in high school, were good hikers. They wore leather shoes and their feet filled those shoes; they didn't have to stuff cotton batting into the toe ends to make their feet look normal.

"I guess," admitted the Westerner, "my ideas are old fashioned and come mostly from Chinatown and the movies. Jimmy here isn't like the picture of a Chinaman I've been brought up on. His haircut is O.K. He doesn't speak pidgin English, and he doesn't look as if he carried a dagger."

That night, after their guest had gone to his dormitory, a special session of the fraternity was called. They would elect Jimmy Chen to membership. The Westerner, far from blackballing his new friend from the Far East, made some telling points in his favor: Jimmy had family background; he was a pretty good athlete; he was a gentleman and he was a scholar. It would be an honor to the fraternity to have him join. "That's right," everybody assented.

But these enthusiasts were reckoning without national headquarters. A sharp letter advised of the ruling passed several years before to the effect that no Oriental would be admitted into any chapter of the national organization. For several weeks Jimmy's friends discussed whether they would resign from the national and start a new fraternity with a spirit more in keeping with the times, or whether they would wait and try to educate their brothers at the convention next spring. When Jimmy got wind of what was happening, he put on a Chinese supper in the home of an American friend who lived near the campus, and invited some of the fellows from the fraternity. There was a huge platter of fish in the center of the table, little bowls of tea, young bamboo shoots, rice and spaghetti. When his guests fumbled with the chopsticks Jimmy laughed and described the first time he had been confronted by a knife and fork. He had been the guest of a young missionary who didn't know China very well. Jimmy said that he watched the missionary take up a knife; he did the same. Then a fork. But, for the life of him, he couldn't juggle those crazy things properly. He realized it wouldn't do to put the knife in his mouth, but how else could he get any potato *into* his mouth? Great beads of perspiration stood out on his forehead. The missionary had asked him if he were ill.

When Jimmy's supper party came to an end he stood up and smilingly addressed his guests: "Gentlemen," he said, "in my country ignorant people, because of unfortunate experiences with a few individuals, say bad things about you, that you're nothing but dollar chasers and imperialists. In your country ignorant people make careless generalizations about us. But in this experience of friendship I have learned that we can laugh together at such absurdities."

On Sundays after church Jimmy would play with the children in this American home where he put on the Chinese supper, and at night would generally go out to some meeting to interpret China. And here is something that sounds incredible, but the host who arranged these meetings for Jimmy vouches for it: in the four years in which he made two hundred speeches before about twenty-two thousand people, invariably Jimmy would say, "I never knew what a Chinese laundry was till I came to America." And almost without exception, no matter how clearly he tried to state this fact, from one to five persons would come up to him at the close of his talk to ask: "Does your father run a laundry back in China?"

Jimmy was not satisfied with making speeches. During the summer vacations he acted as counsellor at a camp in the mountains for underprivileged boys. For the first two or three days the youngsters would shy off and mutter to one another, "Look at the Chink!" Soon they would be clustered around this college man, unconscious of his skin. Before Christmas every year, there would be a reunion with a few of the boys; they would have a good feed and spend the night on the campus together.

The last summer he was in this country, Jimmy attended a conference of students gathered from many colleges. Instead of playing ball one afternoon, he wandered off into the woods alone to wrestle with a problem. That night he stood up before his delegation and said simply that he had chosen Jesus' approach to God.

When his ship sailed, the American friend who had so often been his host came all the way down from his vacation in the Northern woods to see Jimmy off. Jimmy did not say very much, but he placed in the American's hand a letter for him to read later after the ship had left the harbor. This American had sometimes wondered whether his contacts with foreign students amounted to anything. Here for ten years as a student pastor he had been having them in his home and arranging for them to get a glimpse into typical homes, but with what result?

The letter was a reassurance:

On the eve of sailing from your country, which I love so much, to my own people and, my own country, which I want you in time to come to love equally as well, how can I thank you? . . . You helped me to find God as a power in my life. My people need him so much. I return to my country determined to work for that order of society where justice, goodwill, understanding and love for man as Jesus taught it will dominate. You in America and I in China unite with men around the world, working to make the kingdom of God real. To my friends—not good-bye—farewell.

More than a year later two letters from far up the Yangtze River came in the same mail to the American. The first was from an old friend who was teaching biology in a West China university supported by both Chinese and American funds. Jimmy Chen, traveling through that section on insurance business, had burst in for a chat that afternoon. "Remember that beefsteak you promised me? I'm here!"

Jimmy looked older and was much more matured. He was still carrying his idealism with him. He wanted to be a pacifist but it was hard to stand by and see his country over-run. "I would be glad to fight or to die if I could see that it would do China and the world society in general any good." The important thing about Jimmy was this: he was still looking through Christian eyes. The contacts back there in college were not futile. They were blossoming into concrete character, into personality that was worth while. An influence that had sprung from friendship was becoming a force on the opposite side of the globe.

The second letter Jimmy had pounded out on his host's typewriter. After the usual banter, there was an account of how he and his brothers, acting on the inspiration of the boys' camps in America, had surveyed a plot of ground in the hills a few miles from where he lived. They were going to build up a camp for poor boys who never had spent a night outside the old city wall. He had also gotten together some Chinese fellows graduated from American colleges, and they had worked out a plan to show the same kind of friendship to foreign guests as his friends in America had shown them. The other night six American naval officers met with them—"not a swanky affair, just a few of us together around the table, chatting and getting acquainted."

Then followed a description of what the university out there was doing. In the old days some of the missionaries with the best of intentions had seemed to him to be "forcing the Chinese to take their medicine." Now he was able to write:

> I believe that they have realized the importance of changing the method to one of assistance and help. They work with us now as guides and friends. Johnnie and Clinky [his host and his host's wife] are the best examples of this new type. Instead of just preaching, they have a Christlike attitude. And their way of living gets results. It is men and women like these two that we like to see in China. The troubles in China now are mainly caused by the lack of unselfish leaders who should follow the footprints of Christ. It is the university and the people out here that are sweeping and making clear this road for the Chinese to identify and follow.

The Orientals among us are not many. For every six hundred or more Americans or Canadians there is only one Juan, or Mary or Jimmy. But their significance may be far greater than we suspect. They are not a discussion-group topic over which we can twiddle our thumbs and let it go at that. They are rich and vital personalities whom it is exciting to know. They are not abstractions like "the yellow peril" or "cheap labor"; they are a stimulus.

They are a stimulus to carry forward what our missionaries abroad have started. Our missionaries are not agents of the munition makers or the banking interests. They are bridges of friendship. Their purpose is to

speak on behalf of an Asiatic who once said, and
through them keeps on saying, "You are my friends."
In the Philippine Islands they have encouraged in
youth a consciousness of spiritual need. In Japan they
have advertised the blessedness of being peace-makers
and thus children of God. In China they have demon-
strated during Boxer rebellions and communist anti-
Christian campaigns that one is to be congratulated if
one is persecuted for righteousness' sake. All through
the East they have proclaimed and sometimes successfully enacted the spirit of the Sermon on the Mount.

And out of the East have come to our shores these
potential friends who are our opportunity. They are
runners with us in the same race. Whether consciously
or unconsciously, they are children of God; that is,
candidates for perfection. If we can help to remove the
obstacles in their path, we shall be making real the
idea at the center of Christian missions.

But to do this, we must first face several sets of very
obstinate facts. These Oriental people living among us
are handicapped by certain economic restrictions; by
the delusion that, if we are to enjoy a high standard
of living, they must endure a low standard of living.
They are held back by the barbed wire of race prejudice. They are confronted by a glass wall that sep-
arates the older generation from the younger.

Now, they can become fellow-spokesmen with us in

interpreting to East and West "the realm of things in which we share." They can work with us in the most urgent of all tasks that challenges the world today: the task of building a cooperative commonwealth in which we shall all sit down together at the same table of life, with reverence each for the other, and reverence for the God revealed in Jesus whom we discover in our own experience "only as we will to love."

In the following chapters we shall try to see how this can happen, and how, first of all, we can remove the obstructions. We shall try to get an answer to these practical questions: What can we do to share, not the worst, but the best our civilization has to offer? How can we create a new atmosphere so that friendship and justice may grow between us and all who come, or whose ancestors came, out of the Far East?

CHAPTER TWO

THE ECONOMIC TEETER-TOTTER

LONG before Columbus sighted driftwood off the East coast of America,—so runs the whimsical story that Dr. Y. Y. Tsu of Peiping delights to tell when addressing audiences in the United States,—an adventurous and canny crew of Chinese sailed through the Golden Gate and landed in San Francisco bay. One of the party was sent out to explore the economic possibilities of the situation. He returned, shaking his head gloomily. He'd found only a few natives running around in animal skins, not a stitch of silk or cotton or linen on their backs. Then said he, "No clothes—no washee. We go back home." So the disappointed Chinese crew climbed aboard their junk and steered towards the Celestial Kingdom where people wore clothes and where the economic possibilities were a little more visible.

The Oriental who lands on our shores or who was born within our boundaries has just about as hard a time locating a job now as did the Chinese laundrymen of that apochryphal tale. Often his color loads the dice against him. It is perplexing enough for white youths to fit into the economic system. The tired technocrats may still be talking of shorter hours, divided work and everybody functioning in his particular task in an intelligently planned society. Meanwhile, this is the actual situation. You get a teacher's certificate only to be informed a few months after graduation that you aren't needed. Teachers with experience are already a glut on the market. You train for engineering, but after a year of pounding the streets you are glad to fix up the old bicycle and take on a paper route. Or, perhaps, agriculture was to be your contribution. But they are ploughing cotton under, and grinding little pigs into fertilizer. Farmers are being subsidized to grow less corn. Surely it's a topsy-turvy world!

A few years ago youth was all dressed up and given a very definite place to go; they were sent to the trenches. Today youth is all dressed up—to use Mary Yamamoto's phrase—and there's nowhere to go. Bilked then; blocked now. The economic world seems to be still divided into two parts: the suckers and the blood-suckers. And if you're "educated," that means, doesn't it, that you are clever enough to leave the sucker class and go over to the blood-sucker class? "Anyone in the business world today who tries to be human," declared a recent college graduate, voicing the feeling of many frustrated young people, "will end up by losing his shirt." All too many who, in the old days, would be too busy for bitterness are murmuring this long, long thought of unemployed youth: we are not needed; we are a surplus generation.

Now, if some folk with blue eyes and flaxen hair feel as insecure and thwarted as that, how about the fellow whose glands have raised his cheekbones or narrowed his eyes or tinted his face light brown?

The other day George Liu dropped in to say goodbye. George belongs to a prominent family of a West coast Chinese community. I forget how many centuries before Christ his family tree officially registers. He has relatives who love to inscribe beautiful Chinese characters in India ink on rice paper, scholarly comments on what Confucius had in mind when he said, "Within the four seas all are brethren," or what Laotse meant in that famous saying,

> Production without possession,
> Action without self-assertion,
> Development without domination.

But George Liu wears all this background lightly as a flower. It is no issue with him. He has never been in China. He feels American. He acts American. He is American in birth, in schooling, in citizenship. Moreover, he holds a postgraduate degree in commerce.

"George," I asked, after we had talked about the

ship he was to board the following week, "just why are you leaving America?"

"We Orientals," he answered without bitterness in his voice, "we Orientals just aren't wanted here." And he really believed that. He was convinced that, economically speaking, the odds were against him in this country.

"When I applied for a job to help pay my way through college," he said, "they filed my name and forgot all about it. I was just a Chinaman. Suppose I try to get a job as grocery salesman. They would keep me on only so long as I would bring in a lot of Chinese trade. I have a friend who got a job many years ago as teller in a bank. He's still a teller; he won't get promoted because he's a Chinaman. Another friend drummed up trade among the Chinese for a newspaper. Soon after he had built up a good subscription, they laid him off and put a white man in his place. My sister has a fine job in the pictures. We could all move out of Chinatown. But, maybe, the same thing would happen to us that disgusted one of our neighbors. Five years ago he bought a place through a real estate agent. For a while he thought he was going to live out there in peace away from Chinatown. But the Ku Klux Klan got wind of it. They burned the chicken coop in his backyard, chickens and all. They fixed it, apparently, so that the grocery store wasn't anxious to sell things to the Chinese family. Finally stones were thrown in through the window, and tin cans and other things were left on the front lawn. As for ordinary day labor, the unions are against us. We try to be law-abiding citizens but we are not acceptable as Americans. We get the feeling that we aren't wanted. In China there will be hardship. But at least I will be treated as an equal; my ancestry and complexion won't automatically close doors in my face."

George Liu is not entirely typical. Not all second generation Chinese, by any means, are actually buying their passage across the Pacific. But, if you think he is morbid, just get the confidence of some Chinese you know or knew at school; and ask him if he doesn't sometimes feel pretty much the way George did.

What would *you* do? Gravitate to some hand-to-mouth job in a vegetable or fruit market, chop suey restaurant, in a home or hotel as a "boy"? Even some of the ordinary manual jobs are out of the question in California. For instance, Article 19, Section 3, of the California constitution provides that no Chinese shall be employed on "any state, county, municipal or other public work, except in punishment for crime." Or would you do graduate study and aim to deal only with other Orientals in Chinatown and Little Japan, as a doctor or dentist perhaps? You would hardly try the law; for a Chinese or Japanese has a better chance before a jury if he employs a white lawyer. The trouble with professional work among Orientals is that too many white people, as well trained as you, established themselves years ago, and you are too late! Organize a Chinese laundry or a chain of laundries? Don't be foolish; in that little game, steam and the white man will win. Be an "herb doctor" of the old China school? The Health Department might come down on you. Get into an American bank with a Chinese department? But they evidently prefer to employ non-American-born Chinese. As for Chinese capitalists in this country who could employ men of their race in factories or big business establishments, where are they? Importing Oriental bric-a-brac offers some possibilities, but even more competition.

There are exceptional cases where Orientals have jumped over the barriers. In the city engineering department of a large Western city is a respected and efficient Chinese on salary. In another city a Chinese chemist worked with a soap concern until the company failed.

Hawaii, that melting pot in the Pacific of East and West, has less race prejudice and possibly more economic advantage, but to go there is to be pulled up by the roots with none too great a chance of getting transplanted again. Over here, on the mainland, four or five lucky individuals of Oriental extraction are employed by the San Francisco and Oakland school boards. In Los Angeles, pressure from the Japanese-American veterans helped secure for a second-generation Japanese girl a secretarial position in the school system. About twenty Japanese professors are employed in American universities and a handful of Chinese. But for the most part they are not American-born. It is a rare Oriental who can get a job in a department store or hotel or railway office in the larger cities of the West Coast. In the Yokohama Specie Bank and the Japan Steamship Company, responsible positions seem to go to Japanese who can read and write Japanese—an extremely difficult qualification for many or most of the second generation.

Occasional second-generation doctors, dentists, pharmacists, lawyers and optometrists do make their way. In some places it is less difficult than formerly for them to win against race prejudice and build up a white clientele. A new opportunity is opening up for well-trained religious workers in Oriental communities.

Again, Dr. Frank Herron Smith, a superintendent of Methodist home missionary work among the Japanese, points to possible openings in the field of distribution. The older Orientals are skilled producers of vegetables and fruits. If the young people can develop a technique for marketing what their parents grow, that will mean economic advancement. He makes it clear that the openings are probably even fewer in overcrowded Japan than in this country, notwithstanding the success of a young friend who has landed a job in the Yokohama customs office to welcome Americans, and a second-generation Japanese girl who has starred in a Nipponese movie.

Some Americans have a sentimental idea that what these young Chinese and Japanese and Koreans should do is to board a steamer and sail for the Far East "where they came from." The other day a Caucasian student was walking with an Oriental. He congratulated his friend on how lucky he was with his American education. Think of the advantage he would have over the rest of his people when he went back to the old country.

"What do you mean, going back to my old country?" retorted the other. "I've never been there in the first place. This is my old country right here." As for what his classmate called "advantage," he couldn't speak the language over there or read the newspapers. He didn't think the way they thought. Their history was Greek to him. Their customs he did not understand. If he went over there now, he would have about as much advantage as a deaf mute would have over a man who could hear and talk perfectly. If a white-skinned American went across, the people would accept him. They would expect him to make one slip after another. But how about it if you looked like one of them and yet didn't know the lingo; if you had the same kind of nose and cheekbones and didn't observe the etiquette?

Our educational system takes these boys and girls of Asiatic parentage, instils ambition into them and polishes up their training. After that we lose interest in them. They go from one disillusioning experience to another. Small wonder that many of those educated American-born Orientals cry out: "Only in name have we all the citizen's rights; but in fact we are men without a country." And many of us white Americans, when we hear of their difficulties, offer some such glib excuse as this: "If those fellows were settlers in the flood districts of China or had to go with the Nipponese army and get shot in Manchuria, they'd look at America as a paradise." Thus do we soothe our consciences.

Now it is true that your young Chinese in this country does have, physically at least, a far more comfortable existence than if he were the son of an ordinary artisan, say, of Peiping. An American researcher, Sidney Gamble, surveying the living conditions of unskilled and semi-skilled workers in the ancient capital of China, estimates that the average family spends for clothing only 74 cents a month and less than $10.50

a month for food, including 33 cents a year for sugar.[1] These expenditures are stated in terms of the "Mexican" dollar used in China, worth at that time about half of our American dollar. Even in Shanghai, with its sky-scrapers and modern aspect, the average husband's earnings (among 230 working families of nearly five members each, studied by another investigator) are only about $170.00 a year. Many laboring families in the industrial centers are too poor to buy tea; all they can afford is hot water to drink. As for the Chinese farmers, they eat about one fiftieth as much sugar, one fortieth as much animal fat, and one thirtieth as much fruit as the American. And, outside of a few relatively rich homes in the coast cities, where are the children that have milk or butter or cheese to build up their body growth?

In Japan children are not seen lying on their stomachs to smother the pangs of starvation, a little trick that not only Chinese but youngsters the world over seem to learn when the food is gone. But there have been rice riots, and despair is driving many youths each year to throw themselves into the craters of volcanoes or the "smoke" of waterfalls. The struggle for jobs after graduation is even more intense than for white students over here. In some respects economic security

[1] Sidney D. Gamble, *How Chinese Families Live in Peiping*. Funk and Wagnalls Co., New York. 1933.

in the Orient is all too like a raft in a heavy sea with thirty men fighting for a place aboard when there is room only for ten.

Apparently the economic struggle over here is not so bewildering for the old folks who have never done a snake-dance around a field after a football victory, or who have never fretted their intellects over "Psych 203" or "Econ 11." If the younger generation of Orientals feels like a tumbleweed blown this way and that by unemployment, how about their oldsters? Perhaps their roots strike deeper and they can endure a low and precarious standard of living intolerable to their children—though one sometimes wonders how they do it.

Climb out on the rocks along the Monterey coast early some morning when the tide is out and the seaweed gatherers are filling their baskets. Those Chinese have a wise and kindly weatherbeaten look as if the centuries since Confucius were peering out at you. Next month they may be without adequate shelter or a visible next meal, but they keep their poise. A few of the old-type Chinese, like Wang in *The Good Earth,* can still be seen planting or cutting beets, lettuce, onions or spinach in their tiny fields on the West coast. But many have long ago settled within the city limits in their Little Canton, where, around the corner, they can purchase for the New Year and other festivals proper incense and firecrackers and slogans to paste over the door, and proper food: snails, watercress, varnished duck, and those precious eggs with a history that no old-style Cantonese could be ashamed of. Honest folk, so everybody says. Only after several years of depression were a few of them forced to seek aid at the relief centers. It must cut deeply into their pride, for hitherto the Chinese family or the neighbor have always themselves attended to their destitute.

In spite of improved machines and the huge plants common in these days of mergers, there can still be discovered here and there over the country little groups of Chinese carrying on hand laundries. In a farming town of the Mid-west, in a New England fishing village or a Southern city, the inconceivably hard-working and patient Chinese, if you greet him, will break into a contagious grin over his ironing board or kitchen stove, and respond in a word of his picturesque pidgin-English. But good old "Ching Ching Chinaman," of Wilbur Daniel Steele's sympathetic story, although a familiar friend in many places over the land, in far more cases than we may realize has "gone West."

Japanese of the older generation, who were not kept out of the country until twenty-five years after the Chinese were excluded, are mostly concentrated on the West coast and chiefly in California, though New York has a few. They bow and laugh as they hand you across the counter a bunch of flowers nicely wrapped in green paper. They sometimes skid around a corner in the old model T that is always bulging with the hose and rake and inevitable lawnmower. They can be spotted through field glasses in the little motor-driven fishing boats half a mile beyond the surf, busy with their nets. On any long journey through the West they are a part of the landscape, crouched between the rows of Colorado sugar beets or California beans. In the Northwest a few are in canneries or railway gangs or in the mines.

When Columbus first encountered the redskins he imagined they were inhabitants of India. If, today, he should motor through the Imperial Valley during the hot season when the mid-day thermometer touches one hundred and twenty degrees, he would see in the late afternoon or early morning a few real natives of India. He would hear them referred to as "rag-heads," and they would probably be lifting cantaloups into trucks or picking cotton or pitching alfalfa. These upstanding, beturbaned farmers from northern India are used to heat, but even they lay off a few hours around noon time. In the San Joaquin Valley they raise peaches and pears; around Fresno they specialize in raisins. Up in British Columbia it is apples and vegetables. Many of them cannot read and write in English, so they remain socially aloof. In former days when an employer would try to exploit them and not meet their demand for adequate wages, they would move off the job, Gandhi style, without a word or show of anger.

The Oriental who ekes out a living from the soil out West has stiff going. In one instance that happened in the summer of 1933 several hundred Japanese, Filipinos, and Mexicans in Southern California, unable and unwilling to carry on any longer at fifteen cents an hour picking raspberries under a broiling sun, went on strike demanding twenty-five cents an hour. Their employers had the Filipino and Japanese leaders held incommunicado in jail for two days, on criminal charges of vagrancy—the old, old way of harassing those who struggle for justice.

The way we so-called "Nordics" set out to keep the Oriental down under the pretext of holding civilization up has often proved how little civilized we actually are. Not long ago one hundred Filipinos were driven out of Fresno by infuriated whites. In the city where I live the Japanese, about ten years ago, were not allowed to build a church on a certain plot of ground. A great deal of agitation developed around the issue as to whether the proposed church would or would not lower the value of the adjacent property owned by whites. At last the real estate group won; white Christian homes were protected, and the Japanese

Christians had to look elsewhere for a place to worship God. A Jewish friend, an editor of a morning paper, ironically suggested this headline to cover the story: "Keep Our Christ from the Japs." Forty years previously certain citizens, suffering from either hyperthyroid or superpatriotism, had lynched approximately twenty Chinese. Their motive was pure. They didn't want their high standards to be pulled down by foreigners with pigtails.

Not many years ago a lumber mill in the Northwest let it be known to the white community that Japanese laborers would be employed. The Japanese came in good faith. One night they found their homes invaded by a mob who climbed in through the windows and opened the doors from the inside. The Japanese were told laconically to pack and leave. Soon the thirty-five of them were bumping along in a truck, to be dumped with their possessions into another city. The Americans thought they were defending their high wage standard which they were sure the incoming Japanese would corrupt. It is encouraging to read that the Portland Council of Churches, after a systematic investigation of this incident, made a strong pronouncement upon it.

The following dialogue between a home missionary surveying the Japanese situation on the West Coast and a California gentleman on a Pullman car, throws light on the sentiment that prevailed a few years ago and which still festers in certain communities.

Home Missionary: What's the trouble with these Japanese anyway? Are they immoral?

California Gentleman: No, not offensively so. They have different standards from ours, but they are not immoral.

H. M.: Well, are they criminals?

C. G.: No, that is one of the things we can say for them. They are far below the percentage of criminals furnished by the white race.

H. M.: Well, are they dependent on your charities, and are they shiftless?

C. G.: No, that is one thing that they are certainly not.

H. M.: Well, then, what is the trouble with the Japanese?

C. G.: To tell you the honest truth, they are just too smart for us Californians.

When anti-Oriental agitation has reached the hysteria point, some persons calling themselves Christians have acquiesced and even joined the mob. But there are church leaders in the West who have refused to haul down their Christian flag. In 1886, citizens of Seattle became panicky over immigrants from the Middle Kingdom living there. The pastor of a Methodist church was threatened with violence because he was not only for foreign missions to China but for home missions among the Chinese of Washington. But he kept on protesting against the burning of Chinese stores and homes and a Chinese church. His preaching must have had some effect. One Sunday morning he found himself facing a congregation with rifles ready—not for him but for the agitators who had threatened to kill an outspoken friend of the Oriental.

Why all this bitterness and violence? Why have ordinary Americans felt the frost go up and down their spines at the mention of "the yellow menace"?

We cannot understand the reasons why Filipinos in California have to wonder today whether their lives are in danger, or why second-generation Japanese have to doubt that they have any economic chance at all, or why Chinese high school graduates consider permanently departing from the country of their birth, unless we go into the emotional history of "the invasion from the Far East." Because of what happened before he was born, the young Oriental is under an economic handicap now.

The first Orientals to arrive in the United States were probably a handful of Japanese fishermen who in 1842 were caught in a storm off the Japanese coast and blown out of their course. In time they drifted to a desert island where for half a year they heroically subsisted on almost nothing. An American whaler happened by, took them on board, and brought them to the land on which perhaps no Japanese had ever looked before. The hero of this party, Manjiro Nakahama, studied for a while in a Boston school. Nine years after the storm had made him an unwilling visitor to our shores, Nakahama San stepped off his own American whaler to tell the Nipponese about the strange land to the East where the natives put boiling water into a boat and made it go. At that time it was against the law to leave Japan, and any subject who ventured to leave his country was in danger of losing his head. But, perhaps, the emperor's officials thought Nakahama San's narrative too intriguing to silence. It was not until 1885 that the last official ban was lifted and any Japanese who desired could seek his fortune sailing East.

Possibly Chum Wing in 1847 was the first Chinese to take a "look-see" at America. No one seems to know how he got along. He was followed next year by three more Chinese, one of them a woman who became a family servant, the other two going down into the mines. Now, the Chinese likes his own home country; under normal conditions he stays there. But, thanks to the Opium War of 1840—when we of the Occident at the point of a gun compelled the "heathen Chinee" to purchase opium brought in by Western ships, while we Westerners pocketed the profit—the cost of government, such as it was, went up. Then came the Taiping Rebellion, led by a lunatic who seemed to think he was the elder brother of Christ, and before that ghastly struggle was over the cost in lives was alleged to be as great as that in the World War. Taxes soared higher still. So the sober, unromantic chaps in the neighborhood of Canton, who otherwise would have been quite content with their two or three little pigs on the tiny farm, found life altogether too burdensome at the hands of the tax gatherers. And perhaps they also had what youth the world over and through all the centuries has had—a hankering for adventure. Anyway, across the ocean was said to be a mountain of gold. They would try their luck digging in that mountain for three years or so, and then they would come back. How optimistic these Cantonese were who fought for a chance to squeeze their way into the steerage can be guessed from the fact that by the year 1852, just four years after the three Chinese landed in San Francisco, there were on the Pacific coast twenty-five thousand from old Cathay.

John Chinaman, as he was good-humoredly called, for many years was welcome, and sometimes he was able to win not only the respect but the deep affection of some Americans. Dean Charles R. Brown tells of

a Chinese houseboy who came in the early days of
California and went to a mining camp in California.
He had become a Christian. A white miner employed
him and he worked for his boss with selfless loyalty.
A few years afterward, the miner, now wealthy,
brought $1,000 to Dr. Brown,[1] who was then a pastor
in Oakland, for missions in China. Next year, the
miner brought $10,000; he came a third time, again
with $10,000. When the miner's will was read his total
fortune of about $160,000 had been left for missions
in China—all because of a Christian Chinese houseboy!

The white prospectors feverishly following the lure
of gold into the gullies and foothills of California were
in too much of a hurry to take their women along.
But good old John could cook and wash clothes and
do any odd job around the mine, and he would do
all this for forty cents a day. Sure! let him go and re-
work the abandoned mines. We're cleaning up fifteen
to twenty dollars a day. Why should we object if he
makes five or eight dollars? It wasn't long before the
state government was rubbing its hands and making a
lot over and out of John, much the way a farmer
would appreciate a prize hen producing daily a golden
egg. Two hundred and fifty thousand dollars a month

[1] C. R. Brown, *My Own Yesterdays*. D. Appleton-Century Co., New
York. 1931.

was the tax California extorted from these Chinese miners.

When the Civil War began there must have been something like twenty thousand Chinese who were bringing into the American banks their stint of nuggets or precious dust. Some of these eager immigrants took to gardening and to domestic service. Or they made cigars, brooms or boots, or sold dried fish. Or they did the hard work in the vineyards and orchards. On the railroads they made a name for themselves. The Central Pacific and the Canadian Pacific farther to the North were completed on a surprisingly fast schedule, partly because of the steadiness and endurance and docility of the thousands of Chinese coolies employed. Thousands had been imported from across the Pacific by Leland Stanford, and the subsequent development of the Pacific Coast is in a measure due to the Chinese laborers.

But boom days do not last forever. In 1877 there was a drought and the inevitable bad times. White people who before the depression looked down on menial labor now began to mutter against these "furriners" who, with picks and hoes, were taking their jobs from them. A demagogue began to get a hearing with his slogan, "The Chinese must go!" The laborers who ten years before were patted on the back were literally now dodging the rocks hurled at them. Then the matter became one of national politics in Washington, and in 1882 a bill was passed by Congress forbidding Chinese laborers to enter this country.

First the Oriental is invited or at least welcomed, says Professor Emory S. Bogardus, eminent sociologist of the University of Southern California. Then he is encouraged with comparatively high wages. Before long he is bitterly opposed; the white man now sees him only as a competitor. At last nearly everybody is against him—his religion is bad, his idea of government is different from ours, and at the rate at which he is breeding we shall all be crowded out. Anti-immigration propaganda, pretty well organized, now breaks loose. This leads to legislation, and the Oriental group in question is officially excluded. But, after a time, a reaction sets in, and a few of the people who once were bitter wonder whether the poor fellow hasn't had a rather hard time of it. After all, maybe he is a human being.

As you have probably already gathered, the Chinese is now approaching or is already in the last stage of this cycle of attitudes. The Japanese, whom we shall shortly consider, is a later arrival and therefore not quite so far along; the Filipino, the latest of all, is only half way through it.

It would be speeding up this process to suggest that the Chinese, immediately after they were excluded as immigrants in 1882, began to be treated with new respect. They are still in some sections of the country looked at askance and associated with opium dens, subterranean passages, and oblique-eyed mystery. But one senses a gradual change in the climate regarding the Chinese, even on the West coast, in spite of the motion pictures and the cheap novels and the tourists' trips through "spooky" Chinatown. At civic clubs in the very cities where Chinese once were deported or lynched the local curio dealer may be slapped on the back and addressed fraternally as Al or Charlie.

Until recently it has been the Japanese who have had to bear most of the brunt of prejudice. Soon after the Chinese were shut out—though sometimes as many as thirteen hundred a year seemed to trickle in over the line—the Japanese were brought in to do our chores out West. Japanese subjects could not obtain formal permission to leave the Islands of the Rising Sun until 1885, although in 1870 as many as 55 Japanese were in the United States and in 1880 nearly 150. However, within the next twenty years they came flocking in. No less than 12,000 entered in 1900; in 1903 more than 20,000.

In that year Japanese "scabs" were used by the coal operators to break strikes in Colorado and Utah. It does not take much imagination to guess how the white united mine workers felt towards the Japanese in general when they saw Oriental cheap labor used as weapons against them. Perhaps the depression in Japan, following the war with Russia, helped to swell the stream of emigrants desperately turning to California as the Land of Promise. By 1907 there were supposed to be 75,000 Japanese in this country (though the census indicates that there were far fewer than that), and most of them were in California. They probably gave the impression of being more numerous than they actually were, and less able to be assimilated. The rancor ran so high at one time that California citizens were seriously contemplating their right to have a revolution if the Japanese were not excluded from the country. In spite of the President's protest the San Francisco school board insisted that the Japanese children in that city should attend a separate school for Orientals.

This was in the days before "open covenants openly arrived at" were the fashion. The United States and Japan entered into a secret "Gentlemen's Agreement," whereby the Japanese government promised to permit only a certain restricted group of subjects to enter our country. Only those laborers might come, for example, who were to take over a farming enterprise they already partly possessed, or who used to live here and now desired to return. C. M. Panunzio, the author of *Immigration Crossroads*,[1] himself an immigrant, is con-

[1] Macmillan Co., New York. 1927.

vinced that if the people of California really had understood the exact content and spirit of the Gentlemen's
Agreement, we would have been saved bad feelings on
both sides of the Pacific.

Six years later, in 1913, the bitter-enders of California
passed an alien land law. Japanese immigrants were
thus prohibited from buying an acre of farming land.
They could rent a field for no longer than three years.
This hostile legislation in ten years was followed up
with another slap in the face: Japanese were not allowed even to make a contract to purchase a crop of
oranges or berries or beans. About the only way a Japanese could do any cultivating of vegetables or fruit
was to use land owned by his children. If they were
born in this country, they might possess property. This
being so, who can blame the Japanese for having large
families? But, no matter what they did, in Caucasian
eyes it was wrong. If they spent more money on
farming implements and less on beefsteaks, that was
wrong. If they made two beanstalks and one berry
bush grow where only desert was before, that was
wrong. It was damned if you don't, and damned if
you do.

Then came the Exclusion Act of 1924. No one who
has not talked intimately with Japanese in the Island
Empire can have much conception of the significance
of that effort of the West coast to stop once and for

all the feared competition and corruption by Orientals. Chinese laborers had already been barred in 1882. All other Oriental laborers, excepting Japanese, had been shut out by the law in 1917. The Exclusion Act, which definitely and absolutely prohibited Orientals from entering the United States on a quota basis, was interpreted in Japan as a direct and intended insult upon Japanese honor. To the Japanese it was as if the American people had singled them out and said, "We will not have you in the United States because we consider you inferior. We can let in a quota or selected number of Europeans every year, but we cannot tolerate a quota of from 135 to 185 new Japanese settling among us every year. We will admit Negroes of African descent. Mexicans can cross our borders. But you Japanese to us are nothing more than outcastes."

For more than two centuries Japan had been like a hermit, a self-sufficient land, unaware of the family of nations, unexposed to Occidental influences. Then, in 1853, our Commodore Perry with his black ships and threatening guns flaunted the Stars and Stripes in Yokohama harbor and forced his way through the sealed gates of the proudest nation on earth. Seventy-one years later, Japan, sensitive but hospitable and eager to adapt herself to the modern interdependent world, heard the doors of America banged in her face.

No sooner were the Japanese locked out than the Filipinos began to come in. No Filipino could become an American citizen unless he had served three years or so in the army or navy, but as a subject he was permitted to enter. In 1910 there were only a handful, 160, here on the mainland; in 1920 there were a few thousand. But, after the Exclusion Act, they came in such large numbers as to become a "problem." The wages in the Philippines used to be about 40 cents a day. On our West Coast, when white laborers were getting $3.70 a day in the fields, the Filipinos were supposed to be drawing $3.47—which looked like quite a raise. America must have shone before the peon's eyes like a land overflowing with milk and honey, and the American employer as a philanthropist.

It would be pleasant to think that the motive which led industrial employers and agriculturists to encourage the importation of Filipinos was a passion to demonstrate the brotherhood of man. But one fears otherwise. It is more likely that they found it easier to build up a tolerant and kindly and non-exclusive attitude towards the Filipino in order the more easily to break the backbone of organized labor. Neither Chinese nor Koreans nor Japanese nor Hindus would be available in large numbers any more, so why not use these eager, ambitious little fellows from one of our own possessions? Especially since there was a threat to exclude Mexicans also.

Somebody in California would have to get down on his knees and pick grapes and prune the vines, plant the lettuce and nurse along the beans. They came in good faith, did these Filipinos, like the Chinese and Japanese before them, and they did their share of sweating between rows of asparagus and on ladders picking fruit. They took us from floor to floor in elevators or carried our dishes back to the kitchen. The big landowners and the people who flourish on international trade were favorable to them. And, from another motive, the motive of loving one's neighbor as oneself, the churches put in a good word for these lonely and oftentimes exploited strangers from the Islands. But against them were a few retail merchants, the folk who thrive on war scares, and also organized labor, increasingly afraid of more "hands" and fewer jobs.

At present the Filipino is somewhere between half way and four fifths through Dr. Bogardus' series of steps beginning with "Welcome" and "Keep this town white" to "You're not so bad after all." Manuel Quezon predicts that American employers will one day be sorry there are no more raw recruits from the Islands to be taken on for cheap wages. It is possible that economic discrimination and bad feelings may drive the Filipino to leave faster than he comes, or that agitation may slam one more door in the face of a guest.

What we need to remember, whatever happens, is our interdependence.

The greatest delusion from which our present order of society suffers is the delusion that your adversity is my prosperity, that life is a teeter-totter, and that if I am to go up economically, you must go down, and I owe it to my family to keep you down. That is a false picture of life because all of us are organically related to one another. Increasingly we are going to find it impossible to go lone-wolfing it anywhere on this planet. The image we had better get into our minds is not the teeter-totter (surely the Depression has shown how ridiculous that is) but the Alpine rope by which we are tied together. It just doesn't pay to let anyone slip down into the glacier crack.

"Every man for himself and the devil take the hindmost," we used to twitter as though it were good economics. Now we are discovering to our amazement that such complacent individualism spells chaos for our country and for the world. For the more high-powered our machinery, the more highly paid must be those who run it. If the workers are not given enough wages, they cannot buy back what they help to produce; and our money structure goes to pieces. What we want is not exploited producers but efficient purchasers.

This applies to the Orientals among us as well as to those of our own color. They are entrants with us in the great race, and the goal is more abundant life for everyone. We who call ourselves Nordics imagine that we can ourselves make a good record to the extent that we hold these fellow contestants back. But that is a delusion. In the long run it simply does not pay to keep them down with inhumanly low wages and a hopeless future.

And this fact a few Americans are beginning to see. Moreover, some progress is being made. For example, in 1932 our Secretary of Labor imposed on students from abroad a severe legal handicap. In effect the ruling was this: they would not be allowed to work their way through college. As a result there were tragic cases of stranded young Orientals thinking seriously of slamming the door on life. There were also protests from people all over the country, voicing the Christian conscience that demands fair play for the guests who some day will be helping to guide the foreign policy of China, Japan and perhaps the Philippine Islands. Those protests have partially succeeded. Today, for example, a Chinese student can do housework on a part-time basis as an "incidental laborer" earning his keep, or a Japanese can pay his tuition in the university by serving, say, as assistant to the librarian.

In the competition of that race at the Olympic games dollars and cents were no consideration. In this other race the stakes are a life and death matter—daily bread, security against old age and sickness. It is here, more than in any other field today, that sportsmanship in the Christian spirit is desperately needed.

Where men stand in line at employment bureaus, where they apply for jobs as teachers and engineers, where they struggle in the fields for the right to a living wage—it is here that the spirit of Jesus must step in. We are beginning to see that as Christians we can no longer take for granted the economic situation from which these peoples of Oriental background suffer even more than we. The call of Christ to go into all the world is a call to every Christian to reconstruct society.

CHAPTER THREE

BARBED WIRE

SAID the Duchess to Alice, "And the moral of that is—'The more there is of mine, the less there is of yours.'" Such, in less kindly fashion, is the sort of thing we have been saying to our brothers out of the East.

But it is not enough to say that the plight of the Oriental in America rests solely on our greed for gain at his expense. Without minimizing the power of economic rivalry to foster race prejudice, we must recognize other factors such as personal feelings. Is it not too often a case of:

> I do not like thee, Dr. Fell,
> The reason why I cannot tell.
> But this alone I know full well,
> I do not like thee, Dr. Fell.

The vociferous way in which we proclaim such prejudice reveals its emotional rather than reasonable basis. Our prejudice against Orientals is much less a matter of positive facts than of negative feelings.

For some obscure reason, most of us "have a yen"

to be like everybody else and to make everybody else look like us. Why must I insist that anybody should try to acquire my identical nose or cheekbones or freckles or style of eating with a knife? Certainly the Creator, who makes not one single leaf precisely similar to another, doesn't seem to be so much concerned with sameness. We Nordics, who happen at this moment to be pounding on the big drums, are not making all the music to which life marches. In the great orchestra are something like five hundred million yellow players, four hundred and fifty million brown members, and at least a third as many blacks as whites. If we make so much noise that we cannot hear the rendition of their scores, the joke is not on them.

It is a new sense of the ridiculous that we need. Most people who have not bumped around very much in the world really do take for granted that their bailiwick is the center of the universe. Only last century the Chinese emperor assumed that all outsiders were barbarians, mere scum that should do reverence to the Son of Heaven. The Mogul emperors of India used to call themselves the "Light of the World" and "King of Kings." And for centuries the Brahman of India has looked down upon the other Hindu castes. It is still an effort for some Japanese to realize that, even though their history books piously trace their descent from the sun goddess, the Anglo-Saxon is not blas-

phemous when he asks, "What of it?" I have listened
to Koreans narrating with a twinkle how, when they
were youngsters, they ran off from the missionary
holding their noses—they couldn't stand the foreign
odor.

"We are the people and wisdom will die with us,"
is an old and ever-present conceit of the human mind.
Even in the halls of learning it dies hard. Can you
name a national social fraternity or sorority that will
permit Asiatics to join? In 1790 our forefathers voted
that only those of the white race were eligible for citizenship. Quite likely none of them had ever heard of
a Brahman, a mandarin or a samurai. It was not that
they thought of the Chinese as dope peddlers (as for
that, probably no Chinese had ever suspected what
opium smelled like until Occidentals forced on them
opium from India for the sake of profits). It was
simply that the founders of this republic never thought
of their neighbors across the Pacific at all. Was it ignorance, something like that which built up the tradition against permitting Asiatics to become "brothers"
and "sisters" in campus houses? Whatever the reason,
many white undergraduates seem to have the idea that
if birds of a feather flock together, that means that
Asiatics must absolutely be kept out of the nest. But,
perhaps, they overlook the human consequences. Here
is one.

"In my algebra class," a Chinese girl confides, "two American girl friends always worked out their lessons with me. We would have lunch together. We were good friends. One day I met one of them at the beach with her friends. She acted as if she were ashamed to talk to me. She looked embarrassed and indicated that I should not appear to know her. Since that experience, if I meet these girls outside of class I do not speak to them unless they speak to me first. I realize now that the Americans are all right to be friends with in the school, especially when they don't know their lessons and need help. Outside the school they look upon me as a stranger, as an inferior, not worthy to be recognized as their friend. After exams it was 'Hello'—that's all."

That Chinese girl is herself prejudiced, you say. No doubt. But what infected her with prejudice in the first place? Didn't she catch it from the campus passion for conformity, our provincial terror of being exposed to the differences and uniqueness of persons who won't make admirable imitations of ourselves? If her classmates had not huddled so close to the herd, she would not have felt obliged to withdraw into herself.

Recently a sorority girl in a mid-western state university one afternoon brought to her sorority house a Hindu student who was helping her with a League of Nations conference. It was not long before her sisters were excitedly protesting. Why, they wouldn't get any pledges if she kept that up. And one of the fellows in a fraternity was already twitting them: "What kind of house have you got anyway? Can't your women get invited out with American men?" The fact that the non-American in question was of fine mind and character did not prevent her being judged on the basis of prejudices rather than facts.

How do these prejudices become so deeply rooted? Often because we like to generalize from one or two unfortunate experiences and accordingly condemn a whole group. Intellectually you may imagine yourself emancipated from race prejudice. But how about your emotions? Maybe they are all tied up because of something that happened when you were a youngster, something that the surface of your mind has forgotten but which still carries on in your subconscious cellar. You were being shown through Chinatown, hoping to feel gooseflesh, expecting the worst. From a dark corner, that must have been an opium den, a yellow face peered spookily. You had never admitted it to yourself before, but every Chinese you encountered from that time on had a weird aura about him, a menacing air of mystery. Even John, the innocent, old, smiling, vegetable man, at the back door in broad daylight, for an unacknowledged reason, gives you the shivers.

Every time you refuse to draw careless inferences

about another race on the basis of one or two unhappy
incidents, you are helping to solve the race problem.
But every time you label a man who happens to have
a pigmentation different from your own and pigeon-
hole him as merely a type, you are sowing the dragon's
teeth of race prejudice. Probably a crab, mused the
philosopher, would be irritated, not to say apoplectic,
if it could hear us smugly filing (and dismissing) it
as a crustacean. "Look here," the crab would explode
with some justification, "I am not just a crustacean,
I am myself alone." With like indignation a foreign
student remarked to a friend, "We come thousands
of miles to study at this university. And what do you
do? You offer us sympathy. But we do not want sympathy. We want to be understood."

The last way to understand people is to judge them
either on the basis of a single, over-advertised trait that
is said to characterize them now, or on the basis of
certain unhappy things that happened years ago. A lot
of our trouble in the world comes from old pictures
of ourselves, old pictures that ought to be torn up
and replaced with new and more accurate ones. Don't
you often feel inhibited at home simply because the
family and the neighbors don't realize that you are
changing, that you are a different person now from the
adolescent who informed the family at Sunday dinner
in a voice half bass and half soprano: "Thank God,

I'm an atheist!"? Then you recall that unfortunate incident six years earlier, when you ran away from home. As darkness fell, the family found you whimpering on the church steps. You don't want to be reminded of such things. They are not typical. But there they are, snapshots firmly fixed in the family-album mind. It is those scenes the oldsters associate with you. You resent their judging you by such pictures as these? Well, that is precisely the mistake we make regarding Orientals among us.

"The Orientals send too much money out of our country," we complain. Perhaps they did export some gold—once. But let us wake up to this contemporary fact: credit now sent to Japan, for example, enters into the processes of foreign exchange. It thus facilitates trade; we buy their silk and they buy our machines. We do not need to exaggerate the amount of wasteland that the Oriental has made extraordinarily productive in order to make a fully adequate answer to the charge that he has been draining economic power away from America.

Another complaint against the Japanese which still lingers in some minds that have not caught up to the facts is that they have too many children. For a time the Japanese birth-rate was higher than that of white Americans. After the Gentlemen's Agreement of 1907, when the Island Empire pledged itself to President

Roosevelt to restrict the inflow of laborers into the
United States, a large number of women were granted
passports. A Japanese bachelor over here would arrange
with friends across the Pacific to secure for him a wife
from the old country. The friend would send in the
mail a photograph of Peach Blossom, and Ogawa San
would shake his head (the Japanese way of saying
O.K.). In time she would be tripping down the gang-
plank in San Francisco harbor, a red and yellow obi
with the peach blossom crest on her back, her chopsticks and pillow bundled up in her big kerchief. She
was a "picture bride." Her arrival aroused great sus-
picion in the minds of a certain type of American. Who
knew but that she had military designs on the country? Her children would become soldiers. The United
States in the course of another generation would be
overrun with the Mikado's little brown men. While
Rumor is running at high speed around the land,
Truth, so a humorist wittily pointed out, is sleepily
putting on his pants.

What are the facts? For a time these incoming picture brides could be seen in the fields doing stoop
labor with a child strapped to the back. They were
passing on the torch of life with an enthusiasm not
often found among sophisticated city whites. And yet,
allowing for the probability that the official statistics
underestimated the birth-rate, the California State Bu-

reau of Vital Statistics in 1922 declared that, whereas
the average white mother had 2.63 children, the Japanese had only 2.83 and the Chinese 3.26.

According to the United States census, the Japanese
population in this country went up from 1910 to 1920
about 53 per cent, and from 1920 to 1930 about 25
per cent, whereas the Chinese, starting out with 71,531
in 1900, dropped in ten years to 61,639, and then to-
talled 74,954 in 1930. But it should be pointed out that
in 1921 Japanese picture brides were restricted, and
since 1924 they have been entirely excluded. The Japanese are now insisting that the women who once
came in under the Gentlemen's Agreement are fast
approaching the age when they will have no more
children. Dr. Frank Herron Smith claims that in 1921,
when the birth-rate was highest, 5,275 Japanese children were born in California. By 1930 the number
dropped to 2,220; by 1931 to 1,800. In 1930 as many as
49 per cent of the Japanese among us and 41 per cent
of the Chinese were American born. Increasingly it
will be a fact that parents of Asiatic children born in
this country will themselves have been born here. It
will be necessary to go back to the grandparents to find
in the heritage of these children any immigrants direct
from the Orient. And incidentally, voluntary parent-
hood is beginning to gain headway. Despite the old-
country official prayer for progeny "like the luxuriant

branches of the mulberry tree," second-generation couples do space their children.

Another thing that gave Americans a bad impression of Asiatics in this country was the fear that they would import disease. There was a period when the truck gardeners were violating the sanitary laws with the result that tomatoes and lettuce which they produced became carriers of intestinal amœba. This condition is being corrected, as we are increasingly making available to the Oriental our technique of hygiene and sanitation and necessary medical care. You who are "all dressed up" in medical school and wondering what opportunities there are ahead—maybe this situation offers you a place to go.

Chinese dope fiends, slave girls, gambling dens— these are mental images that prevent us from appreciating the Oriental among us today, who is no less antagonistic to these things than we are. It is no service to anybody to be sentimental and to pretend that these pus-pockets have not existed or do not now exist in Chinatowns all over the continent. But race prejudice, instead of being a protection against these evils, only fosters them by driving some Orientals farther and farther into these socially sick areas. If they were given normal contacts with Americans, if enough trouble were taken by Americans to share decent home life with them and provide wholesome entertainment and suitable chances to earn a livelihood, there would be fewer victims. On the other hand, it is absurd to picture all Chinatowns and all of any Chinatown as a festering place, as we shall see in a later chapter.

Our own motion pictures, in spite of such fine exceptions as "Ching Ching Chinaman" and "Son-Daughter," have recently done about as much to fix false impressions in the popular mind as any other agency. If you want to disturb the poise of a Chinese student, ask him what he thinks of "The Bitter Tea of General Yen" or "Dr. Fu Manchu." If you go to Hollywood, ask Anna Mae Wong how she feels about having always to play those subtle, mysterious, slant-eyed parts. "They always put a knife into my hands," she complains.

The mayor of a Western city became so disgusted with having the worst features of old Chinatown presented in a screen comedy that he banned the picture. The prejudice manufactured wholesale by the picture people is not one-sided. The Oriental abroad is learning to despise America in general because he sees on the screen representing us "no man who has honor, no woman who has virtue." No wonder one of America's foremost preachers the other day broke out with the remark, "I can think of nothing so unpatriotic as Hollywood." The National Christian Council of Japan has petitioned American churches to "take every step possible to prevent the continued influx of undesirable American films into Japan. Lord Irwin, former viceroy of India, has said that, after the Russo-Japanese War, the Orient learned no longer to fear the white race; after the World War they stopped admiring the white race; after Hollywood's efficient handiwork they refuse to respect the white race."

The cheap novelettes with lurid pictures on the cover of pulp magazines showing long nails, mustachios, daggers, pigtails, black looks, murders, opium, are on sale at most newsstands and drug stores and they outnumber such magazines of constructive character as *Asia, Travel, The National Geographic.* Our newspapers headline the killings of the fighting tongs (predatory associations for the most part, out to collect tribute and foster vice), but let a family tong (that is, a friendly association of clan connections) give relief to a hundred Chinese who have been out of work and are too proud to go to the county welfare agencies, and not a word of publicity is given to the act. Does your local newspaper, that played up this story of the primitive Filipino religious rites, during which an erring woman was evidently buried alive, ever mention the astounding hospitality of down-and-out Filipinos to each other?

The power of words to condition us emotionally against another race was brought out vividly in 1924, when the Japanese ambassador told the American people that if they passed the Exclusion Act there would be "grave consequences." He was not a dictionary expert. It never occurred to this courteous visitor that our Senate would put the worst possible construction on the haphazard phrase and work themselves up into believing he was threatening America with war. "Give me the right word and the right accent," exclaimed Joseph Conrad, "and I will move the world." Not even the best accent can make "Chink" and "Jap" the right words.

It would be an interesting hobby to collect the foolish questions that well-meaning Americans ask of Orientals. Only a few months ago a Chinese studying for his master's degree was asked by a woman who was taking him to a woman's club at which he was to speak, "Pardon me for asking you this personal question, but when did you have your queue cut off?" He blandly told her that the revolution outlawed queues and that he was not old enough to have one when Sun Yat-sen proclaimed the republic. A young Filipino was asked by a supposedly intelligent American whether the Islands weren't quite close to Cuba.

If you really have the collector's passion, file these myths: "The Japanese are so dishonest that the officials of Japanese banks employ Chinese cashiers." See if you can locate a Japanese bank anywhere in the empire where this procedure has been followed. "The Oriental is sphinx-like; he doesn't have emotions like us." But the Japanese who smiles when he tells you of a tragedy that has happened to him is only desperately trying to spare *your* feelings.

The Oriental has plenty of mannerisms to make him seem curious to us without fabricating any out of whole cloth. Say to him, "You aren't going to stay away from the party tonight, are you?" He might say "Yes," meaning to agree, whereas an American would say "No." Again, if he has a certain cultural background, he may give you the idea he is lying when he is only anxious to make you feel comfortable. We Americans blurt out the blunt facts—or what we hastily guess are the facts. Sometimes the Oriental is less eager than we are to call a spade a spade. His concern may be for your sensibilities rather than his own particular interpretation of the truth.

Even these varieties of custom need not cause negative attitudes. The differences can add to the interest of our contacts. They certainly do not imply inferiority. The positive fact to remember is this: the capacities that count most for civilization may be found in any race. You cannot say that any individual with a colored skin is bound to be less intelligent or more intelligent, less emotional or more emotional, less dynamic or more dynamic, than a white man. Any group is going to have all sorts and conditions of persons within it. One of the most learned philosophers in the world today lives in Peiping, but you will also find morons there—nearly as many as any one of our leading cities can boast. The way people are brought up, the culture from which they spring, will put chopsticks into the hands of one and a silver spoon in the mouth of another.

But this has nothing to do with the question as to how intelligent they were when they were born, or how useful they would prove if they had a chance. A professor in the University of Denver, Dr. Thomas R. Garth, has given thirteen years of research into facts for his book, *Race Psychology: A Study of Racial Mental Differences*.[1] The best guess and one of the most scientific he is able to make about the intelligence of one group compared with another is that the intelligence quotient (mental power that does not depend on training but on inherent gifts) of white people in this country is 100; that of Chinese 99; Japanese 99.

Does this give the white man assured superiority? Dr. Garth is skeptical. He cautiously adds, "Language differences, habits of thought and action, group ideals and attitudes, are all likely to distort the facts or to make the facts as they are actually found at the present time misleading to anyone who is not on his

[1] McGraw-Hill Book Co., New York. 1931.

guard." He flatly takes this position: when it comes to the mind there are no basic differences between races; the white man's mind is not fundamentally different from the mind of the red, black, yellow or brown man. "All races of men hear equally well, see equally well, and are equally sensitive to pain," he says.

A woman's brain does not weigh so much as a man's but that is no indication, let alone proof, that she is not so intelligent. The fact that your head may be long or round has nothing to do, so far as the laboratory can discover, with whether you will be a research clerk or a famous artist or a dictator.

After all, none of these supposedly important racial distinctions—the tinted mask, the outside appearance, the coarseness and abundance of hair—has anything to do with our power to write poetry or become mathematicians, except in one way. Our exterior may give us an entry to culture or it may shut us off from educational opportunities. But the inward power, whether developed or only potential or stifled by race prejudice, is there all the time.

Inherited characteristics may determine a child's future far more significantly than the behaviorist school of psychology allows for. To say that a yellow baby will jump with as much fright over a loud noise as a white baby and that a brown infant will cry no less violently than a Nordic if it feels itself falling, does not demonstrate that all babies are born equal. What counts in the matter of heredity is not the race you belong to but your family line. The deciding factor in biology is not the nationality but the chromosomes of the parents and grandparents.

One of the most recent summaries from a trustworthy authority is that of Professor Franz Boas, anthropologist and former president of the American Association for the Advancement of Science, who stated before that body: "There is no reason to believe that one race is by nature so much more intelligent, endowed with great will power, or emotionally more stable than others that the difference would materially influence its culture."

Why, then, the retort may come, are white people so much more civilized than yellow people? The question may sound sarcastic in view of the present situation in countries where white people live, where wheat is burned while able-bodied persons eager for work stand in long breadlines; where the nations are still heavily armed sixteen years after the futile annihilation of eight million selected men; and where Negroes are lynched. But, granted that we can build a single turbine that can produce more physical energy than all the slave labor that went into building the pyramids; granted that we are less materialistic and more humane than the Orient because we manufacture more loaves with which we can buy hyacinths; and granted that we prolong life and spread information about preventive medicine whereas there is little or no public concern for the men allowed to die on the streets of Peiping;—what is the secret of our mechanical control? Why has China been "backward" whereas the West has "gone ahead"?

An English literary man answers: "The alphabet." In old China, instead of breaking up language into small units such as "a" and "b," they struggled with intricate ideographs or characters that only the highbrows could master. So brains were shifted away from practical matters to pretty word-pictures, and the common people had to be content with admiring the learned who could read and write. It cannot be easily denied that Confucius helped to persuade the sons of Han to respect the past and not inquire too closely into the causes of material things. Once there was a Chinese law threatening with death anyone who dared to disturb tradition with any new-fangled invention.

Dr. Hu Shih of Peiping, who launched the Literary Renaissance in China, confesses, "We have failed in conquering nature because we have paid too much attention to documents." The Chinese thought of gunpowder first, and conceivably it is to their credit that they did not follow all the possibilities contained in the formula! An ancient Chinese proverb says: "It is better to have no son than one who is a soldier." We gave the Chinese a real demonstration, in 1914-1918, of what war means. The Chinese are supposed to be responsible for the compass. They also took the first census in the world. Two Chinese scholars recently claimed that anæsthetics were administered by Chinese surgeons in the third century before Christ. But whether by accident or choice, science passed China by. It passed the whole Orient by.

Somehow or other a bored young man in an Italian church, with a weird curiosity, asked himself why the pendulum of a lamp kept rhythmically swinging during the sermon as it did. An elderly Englishman caught cold and died because he was so curious on a winter day as to climb out of his carriage and stuff snow in a chicken to determine precisely why frozen meat does not spoil. And an imaginative but canny Scot became excited over steam that made a kettle rattle on a stove. And, lo and behold, we of the West destroy yellow fever in Panama, take a flight across the seven seas, reduce famine in India, and arm Japan with guns and precedents for conquering Manchuria.

But our superiority in controlling steam and electricity is not one-tenth as old as China's culture or India's recorded quest for God. Conceivably the Orient may some day outdo us in things mechanical. Meanwhile, the fact remains that it was we, not they, who forged the key to scientific power, which is careful observation, analysis, experimentation, and a passion for checking measured results and checking once again.

But, allowing for all this, there is no occasion for any one of us to be cocky in the presence of anyone from the Orient. You and I are what we are mostly because of the stimulus we have received, and these Orientals are just about as capable of responding to the stimulus that flashes into character or the mastery of mechanical forces as we are. Next to the almost incredible progress of the grandchildren of Negro slaves who now hold Phi Beta Kappa keys is the astounding advance of science and learning in Japan. They now have over there a far higher literacy average than we have. A Hindu researcher has surprised the scientific world with his findings in regard to the nervous system of plants. I met a boy in Peiping who, before he was fifteen, had translated the classics into the new simplified language for the illiterate.

In the last analysis, when we flatter ourselves upon our racial "discrimination," we are only confessing our lack of scientific discrimination. We do not prove that we are more intelligent and capable of progress by telling the world that the Orientals are stupid and incapable of fellowship with us. The assumption that those of Mongoloid features are unable to learn our ways or fit into our civilization or become assimilated may be a superstition rather than an inference from scientifically attested facts. Have we any evidence that they would not take advantage of modern plumbing, prefer new modern cars to oxcarts, respond to employment of brains as well as of hands, universal education and Christian inspiration, if given a chance? Dr. Hideyo Noguchi gave his life on the west coast of Africa to free mankind from the curse of yellow fever mosquitoes. His courage and passion for research were no less real than the courage and passion for research of our own Walter Reed and his colleagues in Cuba, in their earlier fight against this same dread disease.

T. Z. Koo, hailing from Shanghai with his blue robes and Chinese poise, and representing the World Student Christian Movement of Geneva, can quicken on the American campus a hunger for insight into life as effectively as our own conference leaders. Anyone who has attended the annual convention of young Japanese Christians of Southern California (of various denominations) would hesitate to claim that white youth movements show more sincerity or determination to face the implications of Jesus' way of life than Orientals do.

"Yes," says the super-Nordic, "but the trouble is that the Oriental would take too much advantage." You see lurking in his eye that old irrational terror of intermarriage. If we make the Oriental feel at home among us—so the argument of the alleged typical white father goes but is seldom openly stated—one morning I will wake up and find my daughter has eloped with John Leong or Hiro Yamamura or Silvestre Torres. It is all very well for a leading anthropologist to deny that there is "any good reason to believe that the differences between races are so great that the descendants of mixed marriages would be inferior to their parents." That may be a scientific conclusion in general; parents in particular are afraid to invite Asiatics into their homes. There might be a Mongoloid son-in-law.

A famous professor of sociology suggests that more than likely the Filipinos hark back to Spain, China, the Malayan Straits, Borneo and Sumatra,—and even to the cradle of the race. Then he asks, "But how much does it matter what a person's racial ancestors were fifty thousand years ago in determining his worth today and what opportunities shall be his?" An Anglo-Saxon mother hearing this at a lecture might applaud enthusiastically this abstract principle. Then on the way home she would get worried: "But I can't have Jane going to these dances at International House, or meeting Filipinos at the League of Youth; she might fall in love with one of them."

The Filipinos are rather more sensitive on this point than we unimaginative Americans suspect. They recall that the wife of General Leonard Wood found thousands of children abandoned by their American soldier fathers that had to be taken care of by the associated charities in the Islands. A Filipino leader insists that American homes need not fear intermarriage as a result of common courtesy and hospitality. "Few Filipinos," he says, "who are really interested in their country are going to marry white Americans; they each look forward to marrying a Filipino girl and sharing with her the problems of the homeland."

The tragedy is that the Filipinos here are young and sociable and at the same time practically a womanless group. Out of every hundred in this country ninety to ninety-three are men. Since they are denied normal contacts with girls, they often drift into relationships that are not wholesome. We shut them out of our Christian homes and then hold it against these Filipino boys for patronizing taxi-dance halls with unchaperoned white girls. We Americans are quite right in wanting to keep our home life at its best. But to do this, is it necessary to drive, by our own neglect, young Filipinos into places of entertainment that can easily become a denial of all that the home stands for? Why shouldn't we extend to them the fellowship of our churches which support missions in the Islands?

As for the young Japanese and Chinese, they are not looking for their mates across the color line. Life is hard enough in America as it is without the burden of having to apologize to the clan in Nippon or the family tong in Chinatown for being married outside one's own racial group. In a West coast town, a Methodist church group practised the brotherhood they preached. The young people's society had nearly an equal number of Japanese and whites as members. "But think of the consequences," the Ku Klux Klan would cry. Well, there weren't any sinister ones. They had some parties together and some very good times. And a Japanese girl once considered marrying a young American. But they talked over the handicaps. It would not only be unfair to the children, since people in both color camps would be down on them, but it would be jeopardizing the marriage relationship itself. Marriage is a delicate adjustment between two persons. There is no use asking for trouble; it is better to choose a life partner who has one's own family background, one's own cultural traditions, one's own fine nuances of feeling and taste. So they called the engagement off.

At an international house an American college girl developed a deep friendship with a Chinese graduate student. They both enjoyed the same courses in education and world affairs. They were both Christians. For a time it looked as if it would be a thrilling adventure to go with this young Lochinvar from the far, far West and live inside a city wall and see how tactfully she could take orders from a Chinese mother-in-law. Their home would be a stirring example of race amalgamation and of love that is above such things as language and diet and age-old customs of mind. In Shanghai or Peiping or Nanking they could have made a pretty good go of it. But the chances were that they could not pick and choose, but would have to spend most of their years in a less cosmopolitan place. Whether rightly or wrongly, they decided at last it was not worth the candle. They preferred not to be martyrs to the cause of race amalgamation, however noble that cause might appear to others.

There are social prophets who say that eventually there will be but one single race on this planet, neither black nor red nor yellow nor white, but of a color resulting from the combination of all these. Airplanes, automobiles, and the necessities of economic interdependence will bring us all so close together that intermingling of blood will automatically follow, whether we like it or not. Moreover, interbreeding among the races would not be biologically bad, they claim. Therefore it is well to speed up this inevitable process which will eliminate race prejudice by eliminating race differences.

But there is an alternative to intermarriage. As cousins of the opposite sex can be close comrades and draw the line at marrying, so races can have friendly association without amalgamation. They can be trained from childhood each to look upon the other with deep respect but as impossible or improbable marriage partners. Jane dances with her cousin Jim with no matrimonial consequences. Can't she be decent to Juan, who is saving up for a ticket back to the Islands, without old heads worrying about the integrity of the Anglo-Saxon race?

Once in a while an American will do the exceptional thing and marry an Oriental. When this is the case, what is the use of sniping at these rare individuals? After all, marriage is about as deeply personal an issue as there is in life. Mrs. Inazo Nitobe, Philadelphia Quaker, whose husband was the late Japanese international statesman, is quite right in her emphatic declaration: "I didn't marry a Japanese, I married my husband."

It is doubtful whether the wise and humane way to deal with intermarriage is to pass laws forbidding it. In at least nine states Caucasians and those of the yellow race cannot legally marry. In 1933 California officially prohibited the marriage of American women to Filipinos. Some students of the subject claim that these laws make for illicit relationships. Where children result is it not better, they ask, that these children should have legal rather than illegal parents?

However that may be, where is the justice of treating the Oriental as an inferior and shutting him out from economic tasks he is capable of performing, and erecting barbed wire in front of our homes and communities, under the pretext of maintaining the purity of the Nordic race or preserving dykes against some mythical oncoming brown or yellow tide? If there ever was a racial group proud of its heritage, and obstinate against mingling its blood with foreigners "without the law" that racial group was the Jews. Nevertheless, Jeremiah was definite on this point: "Never wrong or ill-treat a resident alien." And generations before him it was orthodox Jewish law to be hospitable to "the stranger within our gates."

Certainly Christianity cannot be maintained behind barbed wire. Economic and social discrimination against the brown or yellow man is not the way to share Christ with the world. It will only convince the Orient that we care more for our white skins than we do for him in whom "there is no East or West."

Now it is the fashion in some circles today to patronize Christianity, and particularly organized Christianity as expressed in the church. Many within the church itself are as sensible of its shortcomings and apathy as are the critics without. But in the face of the negative it is well to look at the positive too; at the creative pressure that the church is exerting in this matter of racial barriers. People with an up-to-date knowledge in other areas of life still cherish an antiquated picture in their minds of the program of the church among Orientals as just a matter of teaching a few hymns and scripture passages for comfort. Such an attitude on the part of these moderns is as laughable as going about in an 1890 style of hat.

Consider some of the things our churches among Orientals are doing for race reconciliation. It is the voluntary church worker who steers the bewildered Oriental mother to the clinic where she can get free medical treatment for her children. It is in the Christian boys' camp that you find Orientals as leaders and Anglo-Saxon boys in a tent chatting most intimately together. It is in the Americanization work of our churches that the Oriental comes to know what good citizenship really is. In a crisis it is the home missionary who goes to court to interpret, not the words so much as the motive of the Oriental confused by our laws.

This work never gets on the front page of the newspapers, but it is potent. "I am against bigness and greatness in all their forms," said William James, "and with the invisible molecular forces that work from individual to individual, stealing in through the crannies of the world like so many soft rootlets, or like the capillary oozing of water, and yet rending the hardest monuments of man's pride, if you give them time." It is just such tiny molecular forces that will one day disintegrate the hardest monument of racial pride.

CHAPTER FOUR

THE GLASS WALL BETWEEN AGE AND YOUTH

THE barbed wire of race prejudice is an obvious tragedy for all with eyes to see. The glass wall of the prejudice that comes with increasing age may not be so apparent, but often it is no less cruel. And half the cruelty of the world, if John Fiske the historian is right, is due not to deliberate depravity but to our stupid inability to put ourselves in the place of other people.

Color aside for the moment, think of the homes you know where the father and mother would give almost anything they possess to have the confidence of their children. They go without vacations, without new clothes and books and more comfortable surroundings, so that their sons and daughters may have a college education. They pay membership and maintenance dues of a fraternity or sorority for which they may not see much reason, yet they would never consider this a sacrifice, since their children seem to think it necessary. There are Christmas and summer holidays

when they would really like to hear from the young
people, now back home for a time, what has been
going on in the "bull sessions" and the football rallies
and even in the classrooms. But a strange inhibition
makes their children dumb—in their parents' presence.
It is not necessarily intentional reticence on the younger
generation's part. The freshman would give a good
deal to be able to communicate his most interesting
experiences to the folks at home. Only something gets
in the way. He thaws out a bit only to freeze up
suddenly, and all that escapes his lips is that it rained
nearly all last week.

Why this wall?

One reason, as was suggested earlier, is probably
the reluctance of older people to tear up their mental
photographs of their children as they were five or ten
years before. There are other unreal aspects of this
attitude. Just as a person growing into maturity re-
sents nothing more bitterly than to be pictured as still
crudely adolescent, so the intelligent Negro often
squirms when he is asked to sing a spiritual. That will
tend to clinch in the minds of the whites their sentimental image of the slave picking cotton for the master. He wants to be considered as he is now, a rapidly
developing person who in no way corresponds to those
faded daguerreotypes in moth-eaten albums so dear to
an outgrown era. Thus, too, sons and daughters chafe

at home when parents fail to recognize in them the vital changes that have made them new persons.

Young people will wear a mask and remain stubbornly reticent until they are convinced that they are genuinely understood, and that their parents seek not "power over them but power with them." On the other hand, their elders will continue to fumble for contacts until they go the second mile and create an atmosphere in which the children will, with perfect naturalness, take the initiative and act at home a little more frankly and directly, the way they do when they are with their contemporaries.

To break through the wall of reticence between age and youth is hard even among those permanently established population groups whose environment and manner of life does not materially change from generation to generation. It is doubly difficult for a group like the Orientals living in the United States. The tension is not alone the ordinary one of maturity versus immaturity; there is the additional strain of Orient versus Occident.

The Filipinos among us do not immediately face this problem because there are only a few of them over the age of thirty-five. In a sense they represent in themselves a youth movement, with no parental roof or autocracy to revolt against. And young Hindus, outside the handful scattered among the universities, are rare since that racial group was barred along with other non-Japanese Asiatics from entrance into the country as far back as 1917. It is among the Japanese and Chinese that the issue is sharply drawn, and its tragic side is apparent when we try to realize how much the family, for centuries, has been a single unit under parental authority in the Orient.

The first point of friction is over the sex mores. In the language of old China there is said to be no word for the kind of intimate and romantic relationship of which our poets of marriage sing. Mencius' idea of the greatest sin, the most unfilial behavior, was not to have a number of children. Underlying this idea is the basic one of ancestor worship in China and Japan. A wife was not a partner of the mind with whom you shared the color and the light of life; she was a means, and progeny was the end. And woe betide you if you didn't have any children. That neglect would doom you to wander in the spirit world begging for rice. But if, in the picturesque phrase of the Psalmist, your quiver was full of children, your descendants would at the proper times visit your grave, do obeisance and leave the wherewithal (perhaps in paper dollars) to purchase all the food your spirit body might need.

In one of those old Chinese families Mrs. Liang was not expected to do all the family reading and bring home the latest ideas; she was "the honorable inside thing." As for choosing his bride as his life mate in the first place, Mr. Liang had nothing to do with such unheard of nonsense. His parents arranged all that through a professional go-between while he was playing marbles, with his five manly little pigtails done up in red ribbon. I remember a college sophomore in Peiping exclaiming excitedly, as if his decision were a bomb that would blow up the community: "I believe in free love." I tried not to look shocked and asked him to explain. "I think," he exploded, "I ought to be free to choose my own wife!" No go-between or parental prearrangement for Chiang!

Woven into the fabric of Japanese culture is the old-time tradition that the son or the daughter is not an independent person but a subordinate member of a family whose will comes first. Your mate is picked out for you: you may not indulge your romantic fancy when the birds of spring are warbling. No, sir, the elders do the selecting. This tradition, in spite of the craving of many youths for romantic love, is not an easy one to break. In recent years there have been several double suicides in the empire. A young Japanese, inspired by Robert Browning's verse—or more likely, the Hollywood screen—will fall rapturously in love with a girl he has surreptitiously met in a tea garden. She, too, is all for this new way of marriage by personal choice instead of by parental planning. But the

family will not permit the match: the group pressure
is so overwhelming that lovers see no way out but
to climb the mountain path and together hurl themselves over the precipice. These double tragedies are
coming to be known as *shinju,* that is, "oneness of
hearts."

Sometimes the most modern-looking, American-born
Oriental hides a conservative streak regarding the ancient matrimonial tradition. Here is Alma, an undergraduate at the University of California who uses a
lipstick, dances, goes to football games, and considers
herself thoroughly American. At the same time she
frankly admits there may be some point in having the
baishakunin, or go-between, select the right marriage
partner—who will probably prove to be the child of
some friend of the family, someone on the same social
level. "After all," explains this exuberant daughter of
two worlds, "this isn't such an old-fashioned idea; it
is in keeping with the best teaching of modern eu-
genics." And so there is something to be said for the
young Japanese-American who announces: "I wouldn't
marry the man my parents picked out for me if I
didn't like him, but I certainly would try to like him.
You can, you know, if you try." Alma has been to
the old country for a visit. Possibly that is the Con-
fucian code cropping out.

One of her friends who has never set eyes on Mount

Fuji or Yokohama harbor betrays a more completely
Occidentalized mind. She congratulates a group of
young American friends: "You don't have mid-Vic-
torian parents but we do. The old folks just can't see
our staying out till midnight."

Although, during the Spanish régime, his parents
saved the young Filipino the worry of choosing his
wife, at present he enjoys comparative freedom in the
Islands. Boys and girl now and then exchange puppy
love notes in the classrooms; it is not considered immoral for them to talk together, as it is in Japan; and
they meet at dances, though it is taken for granted
that a chaperon will be present. As intimated in pre-
vious chapters, it is on this side of the water that the
young Filipino is bewildered in his social life. He ar-
rives here in his late teens or early twenties. Accus-
tomed to social activity, he craves companionship of a
wholesome kind. Since doors to American homes are
closed to him he sometimes drifts into transient and
unwholesome relationships. When he does marry an
American girl, which is rare, the chances are against
him. Of the cases of mixed marriages studied by a
Filipino investigator in Chicago scarcely any promised
lasting happiness.

Happiness in marriage is not an easy achievement
for Americans confused with Asiatic traditions. One
young man born in the United States was taken to

China as a baby and returned to this country when he was a young boy. He went to public school and finally to college; then he opened up a mercantile business. In his way of living and building up friendships he was more American than Chinese. After seventeen years here he returned to Canton to bring back his wife. Their marriage ceremony had been held in his boyhood just before he sailed for America. When he met his bride again he discovered that she could not even write her own name in Chinese. She had never attended school. Even her own language she could not speak correctly. He did not care for her. The poor fellow was desperate. Should he bring her back to America? At last he decided to leave her in the family household in China and send money to support her, which he has since never failed to do.

Into this perplexing situation of conflicting social standards among Oriental communities, comes the comprehending Christian worker, loving the old people still bewildered by the American school, and alert to the demands of the second generation. She is often the medium through which young Jiro or George builds real friendship with Tomi or Lily. And it is to her that they go when the crisis of marriage arises. Too often in our conventional Christian American church, the life of the individual is touched only here or there. In these pioneering church groups or Christian schools, the whole life is often permeated by the Christian spirit radiating from an American friend.

In the West Coast cities there are now a number of Japanese-American married couples in their twenties who became acquainted with one another in high school or college, in the Epworth League or Christian Endeavor Society. Through several years such young men and women have had the intimate, wholesome, social life of other American young people. Their marriage relationship, refreshingly intelligent and happy, contains the essentials of success one covets for all marriages: mutual magnetism, a common cultural background, a worthwhile purpose in life together. Officiating at the wedding of one such couple, I found in the bride's home the ice cream and cake, the clothes, everything, according to Anglo-Saxon standards: perhaps the flowers were arranged more attractively. The best man was a popular almond-eyed United States college athlete who fumbled in his tuxedo vest pocket for the ring as best men always do. The bride was neither more sure of herself nor less shy than if her skin had matched her white train.

Those from the Far East who are among us need all the light that modern science can give them on marriage and preparation for marriage. And this light they are not going to get at home from parents who still live in the old tradition. Social contact is not enough; nor is emancipation from ancient inhibitions enough. These young people need Christian guidance through the maze of wild theories about divorce and "compassionate marriage" (as a dear grandmother of my acquaintance called it). They need guidance rather than silence. They are in a world where "love" is fatuously flashed on the screen and headlined on the front page as if there were no immediate responsibilities and no permanent possibilities in the fellowship of men with women. They need mediators of the Christian ideal who will show what marriage at its best can mean, "the binding that unbinds," the faithfulness that creates faith in life, the loyalty that leads to a further experience of God.

But the glass wall between Asiatic age and youth is by no means merely a matter of sex and marriage. It includes the whole question of culture and custom. "The older generation," declares a young Japanese-American, "is against slang, against the way we talk, against our taste, against our going to shows, against our staying out late at night, against our going without chaperons, and against our disrespect for elders, or what they call disrespect."

To understand our young Japanese and Chinese friends we must realize that at bottom their culture is very much the same. Japan translated to her own soil many Chinese roots. In Japan's schools the "five relations" are taught today as the basis of ethics. The "five relations" have come down from the days of Confucius who lived in China twenty-five hundred years ago. They cover the relations existing between prince and minister, father and son, husband and wife, elder and younger brothers and between friends. The whole atmosphere of the Japanese people, from childhood to old age, is saturated with authority. Ku Hung Ming, a famous old Chinese literary man (who, fourteen years after the revolution which officially prohibited queues, was still defying the westernization of the Far East by wearing that generally discarded emblem of the past), told me as we supped tea that the best place to see the culture of the ancient Tang dynasty is in certain unspoiled communities in Japan. No doubt he was exaggerating, as literary men of all races so often do. But he was right in pointing out the cultural common ground on which Chinese and Japanese both stand.

To a Westerner the thing that characterizes the cultures of both these Oriental peoples is the emphasis on "face." In other words, if you are brought up across the Pacific, you tend to value your public appearance, your reputation, your feeling of self-respect as a member of a family or community, more than your inherent integrity as an individual. Remain a few days within a Chinese city wall, and you become impressed

with the way everybody has to live under the nose of
everybody else. In comparison with so huddled-up an
existence the goldfish lives the life of a hermit in retirement, far removed from public gaze. By sheer necessity the Chinese developed through the centuries the
technique of protecting themselves by wearing what
we would call a mask. As a result one of the most important things in China is to "keep face," that is, not
to lose your sense of being proper, of acting according
to etiquette.

We of the West might jump to the conclusion that
when an Oriental is keeping face he is only bluffing.
Actually he is maintaining what he thinks is character.
Perhaps it is futile for one who has not lived long in
the Far East to try to penetrate into the real significance
of "face." The point is that the attitude has been knit
into the fabric of Japan's social life as well as China's.
"What will the neighbors say?" is ridiculously important to any American. It is sometimes a matter of life
and death to the spiritual descendants of Confucius.
And now that we are becoming intimate neighbors
around the Pacific, it is important that we recognize
and understand "face" when it appears in international
politics.

The older generation of Japanese, and especially of
Chinese, therefore, have their backs to the wall when
their children who know not Confucius come home

from a party in the "wee small hours." To the parents
it is not simply having a good time like other Americans; it is violating something very precious to their
hearts. Doesn't Wong know, when he takes a girl to
a show without a chaperon, that if it ever got back to
the grandmother in the old country the ancestors
would roll over horrified in their graves? Won't Hiro
ever learn that in old Japan dancing is associated with
an evil life? How would you like to be Wong's father
or Hiro's mother and have to meet every day the problems that they face?

The issue between parents and children is no super-
ficial one like chopsticks versus forks. Many of the
younger generation have a fondness for Chinese and
Japanese food—noodles, bamboo shoots, bean sprouts,
three bowls of rice and a highly flavored fish in the
center of the table, or raw octopus and shoyu sauce.
The issue is not whether one should wear sandals at
home or slippers, whether one should sleep in a bed
rather than on the floor, or whether one should talk
Japanese and Chinese or English. Rather it is how one
should look at personality. In the older generation the
standards of the ancient East, especially the five relations of Confucius, still assert themselves. In the
younger generation, that has been exposed to the scientific spirit and the new trend in education and the
Christian emphasis on personality, it is the standards

of the resurgent West that are struggling for expression.

Of course, in one sense, there is no such thing as "the East" and "the West." There are only persons who happen to live on one side or other of a certain artificially drawn line with which geographers like to divide the globe. On the other hand, these two arbitrarily separated areas are still, to a degree, dominated by distinctive conceptions of what human life is and should be. At the risk of appearing to generalize, this must be said: The Orient seems to emphasize self-renunciation; the Occident, self-realization. The tradition of the former is to subordinate the individual; the tendency of the latter is to give him the right of way.

For example, the parents of a Japanese or Chinese expect the son or daughter to marry so that the family torch may be handed on to future generations, the ancestors correctly honored, and the clan thus glorified. But the children, brought up in the atmosphere of a somewhat socialized individualism, want to marry because they love each other and because they wish to be themselves. What matters to them is their marriage relationship in particular, and not all of their relatives and ancestors in general. This spirit is gaining headway, even across the Pacific, in metropolitan communities like Shanghai and Tokyo, where schools and colleges, radios, books, and newspapers of western type, as well as tourists and returned students, are changing the cultural climate.

A Peiping newspaper carried within recent years an advertisement inserted by an aspiring young politician or business man in which he said in effect: "I hereby give notice that now that I have a good job with the government, no second cousins or great uncles of mine need come crowding in on my home to sponge on me. I am not going to take care of any family connections except my own children, my father and mother and grandparents. Nobody else is going to live off me." To the young American this may sound like common sense. Why support the whole clan? To the Chinese elders this is wild-eyed radicalism. The family, linked by common ancestors, is a unit in all its branches. Isn't it the obligation of any successful member of the clan to share his prosperity with unlucky kinsmen who may want to live under his roof? Suppose you get a good job in famine relief. It is not considered graft, if you line your nest and let your nephews warm themselves with some of the feathers. It is being loyal to the family. Over against this group spirit, in which the individual counts little, stands youth with a shocking demand for self-assertion, for personality first and family second.

A Chinese girl studying in an American university claims that there is more misunderstanding and an-

tagonism between the Orientals and their parents than
there is between young Orientals and young Americans. Apparently the conflict is over freedom of choice.
The parents want to make decisions for Leong Junior
and Hisako. Leong Junior and Hisako insist on making decisions for themselves. Only in this way can they
become personalities, for personality grows when you
face a fork in the road, and decide for yourself between
the path that is difficult and dangerous and the broad
road that is conventional and easy.

These young Orientals have been more or less in-
oculated in our schools against what John Dewey
called the "echo disease." They are in a new world,
and the ancient road maps seem to them of little use
as they grope their way. The "look backward" of Confucius strikes them as less intelligent than David Starr
Jordan's, "The only way out is forward." Some of them
have been infected with the new educational idea that
the most important thing in the world is for personality to grow, and that it can grow not by conforming
to old patterns but by tackling new situations. They
want to get facts, and then judge for themselves what
they should do in the light of those facts, instead of
blindly following outworn tradition that never was
confronted with airplanes and radios, voluntary parent-
hood and war resistance, the municipal ownership of
light and power, sickness and old age insurance.

There are a few of the second generation who, after traveling in the lands of their ancestors, perhaps, come to appreciate some of the old values. Listen to this admission which James Y. Mochizuki makes to his high school teacher in Los Angeles: "I know hundreds of fellow Japanese, both boys and girls, who would give anything to be able to read, write or even speak Japanese. It is my firm opinion that it is the duty of the parents to keep some trace of the ancestral customs alive in one. I was born in this country some fifteen years ago. Born in an American neighborhood, I found all my childhood friends to be Americans. There were no Japanese within the radius of one mile of our home. I remember faintly my mother telling my sister and me nursery tales based on Japanese romance and fables. I loved to hear stories of medieval heroes and leaders. Masashige Kusu-no-ki was in my mind the kind of real man I'd like to be. He fought and died for our emperor, dying by his own hands rather than be taken by his enemies. Such stories made my heart want to go and live in Japan."

As a youngster James visited Japan. He saw his grandparents and was taken on pilgrimages to the ancient temples of Buddha with their sacred pigeons and quiet pools full of golden-tinted carp. It was pure romance in his childish eyes. It seemed to him that in parts of the islands, where Western civilization had not

taken root, the people hardly knew what sorrow was.
There he felt "at ease and at home." There was no
racial superiority. It thrilled him to gather mulberry
leaves in the groves and then, back at his grandfather's
house, listen to the silkworms as they chewed on the
tender leaves. He played and ran races with the other
children who at first laughed at the "Yankee Japanese." They teased him about his hair, so he had a
barber shave his head.

When James returned to this country he was glad to
be back, but for a long time he felt misplaced and
lonesome. His English did not come back for almost
a year. At the school he heard insulting remarks from
the young Americans. "Little did they remember that
they, too, were sons and daughters of people who had
crossed the ocean and had come, like us, to live and
to be educated in the same country." His parents, after
school hours, sent him to the Japanese language school.
"Now," he says, "on bended knees I can thank my
mother and father for giving me a chance in the days
to come. It was they who kept the old Japanese tradition in me." He finds one part of his nature drawn to
America, "the land of our birth, where we grew up
and were educated"; the other to Japan "with its arms
calling and pulling us, the land where our ancestors
were born and were buried."

One can't pigeon-hole the attitudes of these young

people towards the Oriental tradition and the Americanizing process. They range all the way from the giggling high school girl who outdoes the typical ignorant American tourist in her arrogant disregard of Oriental art and culture, or the flippant undergraduate who thinks that a car and a coonskin coat and a pipe are sufficient tokens of being an American, to the thoughtful appraisal of a young Christian Asiatic who says, "Too often we don't know the right kind of Americans." He wants his group to assimilate the very best of the Western civilization, but is skeptical about the value of completely discarding the old. "The modern dances," he says, "for so-called Anglo-Saxons, with their background, have no sinister implications. For us, with our peculiar heritage, they carry real risks."

Thus it is a double life which the young person of Oriental ancestry leads whether he knows it or not. Outside he motors, hikes and uses slang, but the moment he enters the front door of his home, as one of them puts it, he "has sailed five thousand miles across the sea, to a world that is almost a memory among his elders."

Listen to this Chinese mother's complaint: "These Americans teach the children as young as four and five years old to walk in pairs, one boy with one girl. The fathers give their children too much money to spend on parties. The children don't respect either their teachers or their elders."

Let us try to put ourselves in the place of one of these Oriental parents. The mother hears her sixteen-year-old son ridiculing the old family customs. "Henry," she hears him confiding to one of his contemporaries, "everything's so slow down here in China-town. The old folks always just sitting around on the sidewalk; nothing happens." But this son knows nothing of what glows in his mother's heart. To hear him talk you would think that he himself had earned all this new knowledge about driving an automobile truck or turning on the radio, or playing basketball. But he didn't pay for it; it was his father who for the last thirty years had kept long hours in the curio store trying to make ends meet, so that this son of his might get the very best.

And the father—he often wonders about this wife of his and how she likes being treated as a fixture, a sort of family shrine, but with whom you do not really talk. After all, she never as a child had her arches and toes crushed so that a three-inch silken shoe would fit her foot. She can walk ten miles, he muses proudly, ten times as far as the old-style Chinese woman. And she is not like those American women who play cards when they are not fondling a Pekinese or having their faces massaged. She's too busy cooking and mending for nonsense like that. But maybe she feels a little out of it, too, just the way he does, when the children slip out after supper without doing the dishes or stopping to chat, and then are off to spend the evening in somebody's car.

One of the most poignant things I have ever seen was in a shack among the celery fields outside our town. A Japanese-American girl had called to discuss a student problem, and my wife and I, since it was late in the afternoon, insisted on motoring her home. The girl was reluctant to the point of embarrassment. We did not realize why, until after we had crossed a rickety bridge over an irrigation ditch and bumped along an impossible byroad and parked in front of her home. The girl called across the field to her mother, for the father was already on his way to market.

When the eager little woman trotted up to us and bowed and bowed again, the contrast in appearance between her and her daughter was unforgettable. There stood the new generation, tall, slim and manicured, spick and span in white oxfords, muslin and Easter hat: she would not have been out of place on Fifth Avenue. Beside her stooped the older generation, hands calloused and soiled, boots and cotton skirt covered with mud, skin weatherbeaten like the unpainted boards of the shack. It would never occur to her to borrow one of her daughter's dresses and go with her in the bus to a lecture on psychology or philosophy at the great university six miles away. Nor would the thought disturb her that she was cut off from such expanding horizons.

On the contrary. She was glad to give all her waking hours to tending the tiny celery field which her daughter (as an American citizen) owned, because Alice could stand on the mother's shoulders and learn all that America could offer. What matter how simple the food? Or how keenly they longed to lay off work some spring and see the thatched houses once again, the cherry blossoms and the eternal snow on Fuji-San? That tired little figure, urging the daughter to interpret in English, who warmly welcomed us to her home, in the dusk took on a strange nobility. Rough and unlettered, on the outside, she was of the soil. But one sensed that on the inside there was a hunger for life, and an ardent spirit. Next morning, when Alice would be taking notes in the classroom, the mother would be kneeling among the young celery plants, her thoughts, perhaps, far away across the sea, dwelling among the times of her girlhood. Americans speeding down the boulevard unable to see what we had glimpsed the evening before, would point with disgust: "Look at that Jap. People working that way all the time and living on nothing are a menace. We ought to ship them back to where they came from."

It is in religion, in the relationship of each unique soul with God, and the demand for a social order less contrary to Christ's spirit, that the older and younger generation least understand each other. Alice's mother is probably a Buddhist. That is, if anyone in the family should die, she would want the Buddhist priest to take charge of the funeral. The little, gray-haired lady would be shocked if Alice told her that her professor of comparative religions asserts that the founder of Buddhism was against having idols in the house and that he didn't believe in God. She has never had any occasion to look critically into the scriptures which her brother, in a monastery located in a valley underneath the sacred mountain of Japan, drones faithfully every day. But, ever since childhood she has loved the memory of incense, of red- or yellow-robed figures that bowed reverently as the temple bells clang among the cryptomeria trees.

But this daughter of hers won't ever go to the rather squalid Buddhist temple in the city. She refuses to sing "Buddha Loves Me, This I Know." She has contempt for what she calls "the apple-polishing technique of the priest" who passes out chocolate bars to children who attend his Sunday school. Alice belongs to the League of Youth. She goes to conferences where young people come together from all the Japanese communities to talk about Jesus and pray for the courage to follow him. She doesn't say this to her parents, because Alice rarely tells them what she is really thinking about, but to her intimate friends she confides: "The old folks take their religion as second-hand tradition. We want first-hand experiences. They trust to magic. We think of God as working through scientific law. They repeat formulas. We try to open our lives to God so that he will give us strength and wisdom to put our faith into practice. They say 'Buddha, Buddha' and look to heaven. We would like to do Christ's will in the world." Alice might not use these exact words, but they would indicate her general idea.

How many Buddhists there are among the Japanese in this country would be difficult to determine. The latest statistics give 7,000 as connected with the Buddhist mission in America.[1] Of the 66,000 Japanese who are not American born, it has been estimated that perhaps 25,000 claim at least nominal adherence to Buddhism in some form. The proportion of Buddhists among the 73,000 American-born Japanese would undoubtedly be very small. About 20,000 children and young people are in Buddhist Sunday schools which, in addition to giving religious instruction, in some places conduct dances, debates, oratorical and athletic contests. Without belittling what the Buddhists are

[1] From "Statistics of the Religious Bodies and Groups in 1932 in the United States," compiled by George Linn Kieffer, *Christian Herald*, July, 1933.

doing to instill reverence and the habit of meditation, it is safe to say that the more intelligent younger people are inclined to be skeptical and apathetic about this faith of their fathers.

The number of Christians among the Japanese who have not been born in this country is thought not to exceed 6,000. It must be recognized that the services held in their churches are often too formal and old-style to attract those who have reached adolescence. An American visiting one of the sixty Japanese churches of seven different denominations might be disappointed at the morning service to see only one or two young people present. But it would not be safe to generalize from one visit. Let him go to a certain church on the West Coast at half past seven in the evening and he will be surprised to discover the entire service of worship managed and attended by the young people, numbering perhaps sixty or more. They sing with an enthusiasm that would put some Anglo-Saxon groups to shame. They share fresh and genuine religious experiences when they talk, instead of parroting the opinion of somebody else, and they pray with sincerity. The brief communion service shows a spirit of dedication. A young American sits through the meeting to help them in any way they wish. He is not a white man telling them what they must do, but a fellow seeker with them. Religious imperialism is beautifully absent.

If young people today are to find their life's direction they must have intimate comradeship, and they must have a challenge to express the Christian spirit in their own terms. In the Junior Church of Christ at Monterey twenty-four Japanese, seventeen to twenty-one years old, are meeting this need in an even more thorough-going way. Until they launched out on their fine experiment in 1931, religion was not very real to them. They dutifully attended the local Japanese church conducted by their elders. But the language was "hard for us to understand; it was classical Japanese. The preacher would use big words like 'congregating' instead of 'getting together.' The problems talked about were not our problems."

So with the help of a young American who coached their basketball team, they organized a Christian fellowship of their own, a youth church within the older church. They chose their own board of deacons and session and arranged to have their service of worship at a different hour from the one attended by the first generation, but in a thoroughly cooperative spirit. The chairman of the executive committee is a cobbler recently graduated from the local high school. But most of the members are fishermen. From October to early March—if there is no moon to outshine the phosphorescent ripple of sardine schools—they work most of the night in the boats that sometimes in one haul net

thirty-five tons. An American coming in tired out on
an early Sunday morning would probably take a good
snooze and let church go. These fellows, if they possibly can, are on hand. They take their Christianity
seriously. And they pay their way. Practically all the
current expenses of the church, excepting the pastor's
salary, are covered by these young men and women
from their own well-organized, every-member canvass.
The plan of this autonomous youth group is working
so happily that other Japanese churches are following
it. There are frequent joint meetings of the older and
younger groups. Here is what promises to be a partial
solution of the conflict between age and youth, with
its happy blending of the experience of the one with
the enthusiasm of the other.

CHAPTER FIVE

GIVE-AND-TAKE

"NOTHING passes between donkeys but kicks," says an ancient proverb. Between East and West there pass frequent kicks, but also something else.

Let us look at the kicks first. We send dollars abroad. Then we get the foolish idea of putting cannon behind them. We want markets or raw materials outside our borders. Then some "hundred-per-center" has the notion of planting a flag where these advantages are, or marching the marines up and down in front of them. That, our historians tell us, is a primary cause of modern wars.

The cure is that we stop being imperialistic, that is, too eager to seize control of land, banks or governments beyond our own boundaries. But to stop being imperialistic we must learn to limit our nationalism; we must practise cooperating with other nations in putting law above violence, even if it costs something. But to become less nationalistic we must learn to watch and curb the propaganda of profiteers who make money out of war and preparation for war. This brings us to

the traffic of the munitions makers which, from the
human point of view, is the most asinine form of business intercourse between nation and nation and between East and West.

Three recent books[1] contain well-documented facts
about the "munitions internationale." During the
World War, we are told, British soldiers in the Darda-
nelles were mowed down by Turkish artillery pur-
chased from English armament firms. Within the past
few years, Germany has armed herself in part through
vast purchases which have enriched French stockhold-
ers. Facts such as these are being given widespread recognition. But this trade is not confined to Europe; it
is being carried on between East and West.

According to the New York *Herald Tribune* of
February 28, 1933, a Chinese and a Japanese purchasing agent happened to meet in the waiting room of a
British arms factory. They compared notes and found
that they were both paying too much for the munitions they were ordering. So a joint ultimatum was
issued, and they won a cut in prices of forty per cent.
. . . Shanghai has become a port where European
arms and munitions are landed. Some are transshipped
to Japan, so that Chinese young men may be blown to

[1] Beverley Nichols, *Cry Havoc!* Doubleday, Doran and Co., Garden
City, New York, 1933; A. Fenner Brockway, *Bloody Traffic*, Victor Gollancz, London, 1933; F. C. Hanighen and H. C. Englebrecht, *Merchants
of Death*, Dodd, Mead and Co., New York, 1934.

pieces, some to the Chinese armies so that Japanese young men may die for their Emperor, or to Chinese warlords that Chinese peasant soldiers may die in futile civil wars. Thus the whole devil's trade forms a vicious circle of butchery.

Perhaps a local airplane factory is taking on some more workers and you are going to get a good job there. Remember Henry Chang that used to be studying in the aviation school? He is in the air force now in China. The airplane you will be making may be profit for you, but sudden blazing death through the air for Henry. Or you may be getting a little extra money from an uncle to help you through college. It comes from his investments in corporations that export chemicals, or steel, to a Chinese warlord. Perhaps you heard that a Japanese high school mate, a fast basketball forward, who returned to a teaching career in his homeland, ended in Manchuria with a bit of America's steel in his chest?

If we can learn anything about this sort of give-and-take between East and West, it is this: in the long run the kicks don't pay. We are too closely interrelated. The papers may seek to boost their circulation by fomenting war scares about Japan. But the last thing the farmers of Japan can afford is to be cut off from marketing their silk in the United States. Japan must sell from eight- to nine-tenths of her raw silk to us;

in return, she is glad to buy cotton, automobiles, building materials, machines and petroleum from us.

"Some years ago the textile mills of New England were closed. Why? Because the usual orders from a section of Korea failed to arrive. Why? Because the hair net industry in that part of Korea had suddenly ceased. Why? Because the American women had bobbed their hair!" This is a picturesque way of describing our interdependence, although most students will admit that the economic problem is much more complicated.

But the fact remains that we need Oriental materials and skill, and they need ours. The exchange of goods does not need to eventuate in kicks, regardless of the press and munition workers that profit from war scares. While being realistic about the possibility of war arising from our economic rivalries, we can use all our imagination and organizing power to build up the agencies that make for international solidarity.

There is already this kind of positive interplay, a contagion constantly passing back and forth, and this is the contagion of understanding. It is a story both new and old.

It was not only the little runner Takenaka who won recognition and admiration at the Olympic games. Every athlete who carried through the spirit of good sportsmanship helped to spread this contagion of understanding, whether on the cinder track or in the swimming pool where the two fourteen-year-old schoolboys from Nippon threshed their way through the water well ahead of Americans larger than themselves. Those who think the Oriental too sluggish to match our skill might ask any Washington schoolboy about Frank Yama, varsity end on the Washington eleven, or listen to the enthusism of West Coast sport fans for Ted Ohashi of the International House, Berkeley, who was the guard in California's basketball team, or Toribio, recently of the University of Southern California, who did six feet eight inches in the high jump before leaving the Philippine Islands, or "Speedy" Dado, perhaps the most famous living bantam-weight boxer.

Every contribution made in terms of character and personality helps to circulate understanding, and often has far-reaching consequences. There is an Aladdin-like quality about the story of a humble Chinese servant who acted as handy man to an American forty-niner, General Horace Carpenter. The American was so impressed with the Chinese servant's character, and became so interested in Dean Lung's background, that he donated one hundred thousand dollars to Columbia University for a chair in Chinese to be named in honor of his servant. When the General died he left a generous legacy to his cherished friend who spent his last years peacefully in his old Cantonese village. Today, if you are planning a business or professional career in China, you need not be illiterate about that great civilization. Columbia offers you scholarly courses in Chinese language, literature and culture. Who can measure the contribution to world understanding made in this way—through the life of a simple servant?

In that same university Dr. Hu Shih won a prize essay contest on world peace. He is that returned student who became famous as leader of the literary renaissance of China. But he has made another contribution. He has helped to unfold to the world the mind of the Chinese philosopher Moh Tih. One suspects it was contact with the mind of the Peacemaker of Galilee, encountered during student days over here, that opened the young scholar's eyes to the value of Moh Tih. The name Moh Tih (sometimes spelled Motze) may convey little to you now, and until a few years ago it meant little more to the Chinese. But, increasingly, the man of that name may emerge as a significant force. He lived centuries before Christ, and was buried and forgotten under the writings of Confucius and Mencius. Probe into Moh Tih's mind, and perhaps you will see why the classical scholars unconsciously shrank from his demands. This, approximately, was his challenge to China: Don't waste money on funerals. Spend your money on living, not on dying. Analyze causes and don't merely pore over other people's documents. Practise love equally for everybody. Whereas the sophisticates condone mass murder you must prevent it. Moh Tih said:

Killing one man constitutes a crime and is punishable by death. The killing of ten men makes the crime ten times greater; similarly the killing of a hundred men increases the crime a hundred fold. All this the gentlemen of the world unanimously condemn and pronounce wrong. But, when they come to judge the greatest of all wrongs, the invasion of one state by another (which is a hundred thousand times more criminal than the killing of one innocent man), they cannot see that they should condemn it. On the contrary, they praise it and call it "right." Indeed, they do not know it is wrong.

Moh Tih was not content with announcing a principle. He heard of a state engineer who was planning war on a neighboring kingdom to try out a newly-invented ladder that would enable soldiers to scale the fortified walls of cities. Moh Tih did not wring his hands and cry, "How awful!" He spent the next ten days, his feet bleeding and dusty, walking as fast as he could till he found the state engineer. Then, in a long interview, he opened the would-be militarist's mind to the enormity of the crime of invading another state and to the necessity of being reasonable and humane. That was too much for the state engineer. "I wouldn't take that territory," he finally bowed, "if they gave it to me."

Moh Tih's principle of Universal Good-Will has been given practical expression over and over again among Chinese in this country. In the Chinese section of New York City is an old building that for many years was used as a mission church. With his seven daughters and sons who were to become well-known, the pastor, Huie Kin, for many years made this one of the brightest spots in the relationship of East with West. It was there that Sun Yat-sen, the George Washington of China, wrote the first draft of the constitution for the yet unborn Chinese Republic, aiming at freedom from imperialism for one-fifth of the human race. It was there that eager-minded young students, the pick of China, would come during their weekends to teach Sunday school or direct young people's work. One of these, "Jimmy" Yen, married one of the pastor's daughters and is now head of what is probably the most significant educational enterprise in the Far East, the Mass Education or "Thousand Character" Movement whereby millions of people who otherwise would be illiterate have learned to read and write. Other visitors, preparing for their careers as professors, married into the family and their homes are now centers of Christian influence in China.

The story of Huie Kin, who died in 1934, is one of

the romances of international and inter-religious understanding. His boyhood was typical of the Chinese who ventured from the small farm villages of southern China to America to find their fortune. In his quaint *Reminiscences,* published in 1932, he describes the two-roomed thatched home made of sun-dried brick. In one room he and his father slept with the family cow. Near the door was the god who protected the house from evil; above the stove the kitchen god—red paper figures pasted on the wall. Two brothers slept in the ancestral temple; the sisters, with their bandaged feet, in a little house by themselves. At the village shrine he used to look with reverence upon the wooden tablets representing the ancestors. His recreation was kite-flying. His job was to guard the cows at pasture during the day. At harvest time the boys enjoyed three full meals: rice, yams, sweet potatoes and green vegetables. In the ancestral hall by the gate of the village, he could recite, with prodding from the teacher's ten-foot bamboo pole, the *Four Classics.*

"Once a cousin came back from a far country. We all gathered around him and eagerly heard him tell of strange cities, of people with red hair and blue eyes, and of solid gold nuggets in the mountains." From then on young Huie dreamed of "Old Gold Mountain," that is, San Francisco. Thirty dollars—thirty of those white round disks of silver—was the minimum steerage fare. The father borrowed them; no doubt the son would return with pockets full of beautiful gold pieces; and the family would no longer have to go without shoes or wear rough homespun. One spring morning the fourteen-year-old boy started out with three cousins before daybreak, lest they should hear the neighbors saying unlucky farewells which might spoil their voyage. In their bamboo basket they carried their worldly possessions and mother's homemade biscuits. During the two months at sea Huie realized that "the fiery-haired fellows with the blue-grey eyes" were as human and admirable as his own people.

At last, on a clear crisp September morning in 1868, he sighted land, the Golden Gate. Looking back on that great day from his old age he wondered whether the ecstasy before the Pearly Gates of the Celestial City could surpass that thrill of arriving. Before long he was looking for work in San Francisco's China-town. A few years previously the Chinese immigrant had been valued because he was helping to open up the vast hinterland of the West through his labor on the railroads. But soon, thanks to crop failures and reduced output in the gold mines, he was coming to be looked upon as a rival workman, the mysterious Chinaman whom white men should dread. Agitators in open-air meetings were becoming oratorical: "There is no means left to clear the Chinaman but to swing

them into eternity by their own queues, for there is
no rope long enough in all America wherewith to
strangle four hundred millions of Chinamen." Children spat upon Chinese in the streets and called them
rats.

Huie's first job was as general houseboy. Every day
there was apple sauce, apple sauce. He was so home-
sick he swallowed a bit of earth from China, mixed
with water, which comforted him for a time. Then
he became a farmer, churning milk, picking berries,
laying water pipes. Later he worked for a Christian
family in Oakland, and then he was in clover. The
mistress taught him to read and write. He was encouraged to go to Sunday school and attend an evening
class. In the neighborhood were a Congregational
church, a Presbyterian church and a Baptist church.
Huie was so enthusiastic he registered in the Sunday
schools of all three, which kept him running from
one to the other all the Sabbath day. He confesses that
his motive was to acquire not religion but language.

Once he had qualms. Could one be loyal both to
the hallowed wisdom of Confucius and to Christ? The
problem was solved through the friendship of a six-
foot scholarly American pastor who invited the boy to
join a small study group in his church and showed
him he could serve his people best by becoming a
Christian. This American finally arranged for Huie,

now twenty-six years old, his queue hanging down his back, to pursue his education in a seminary for the Christian ministry in Ohio.

In time Mr. Huie Kin became a pastor in a mission church on the edge of New York's Chinatown. He tilted with the Chinese gambling bosses and had two or three narrow escapes from their plots to kill him. The daughter of an American manufacturer used to visit his mission, and Huie used to attend the prayer meetings in the school where she was a student. When he asked the father for her hand, the old gentleman was kindly but perturbed. "Have you considered where your children would stand? Yes, his daughter and prospective son-in-law had looked ahead; they would bring them up to be the equal of any other young men and women. Judging from the successful marriages of their daughters years later and the careers of their sons, two of whom are engineers and one a publisher, they kept their word. Their home became famous for its blending of manners and ideas, American and Chinese.

After his retirement the Rev. Huie Kin returned to his old home in China for a visit. A railroad took him to the very doors of the village. The man who built the line was a Chinese who, in the sixties, had been a foreman on the Union Pacific! He had connected his village with the great outside world by raising the money among his countrymen working in America and purchasing from the New York Third Avenue Railway its discarded steam engines, and then single-handed put the job through on Chinese soil with what Americans like to think is their own peculiar verve.

In the Chinese community of our largest metropolis is a Korean physician whose life illustrates vividly the give-and-take between East and West. Dr. Chiang-sei Kim is employed as a public official. He is organizing a health center and teaching the people to open their windows, clear away the garbage and intelligently resist the white plague. He brings to the job rich experience of building up an anti-tuberculosis association and educating for public health in China.

This is how he got started. One day in the Land of Morning Calm, the boy swallowed his prejudice against foreign devils and became a pupil in the mission school. His ambition was to be a doctor. At last we see him in this country, without financial backing but with a well-built body full of vitality and a disciplined will. There is a wife to take care of and children. He sells books. Five times he crosses the continent in this work. Within eight months he has cleared enough to buy a small grocery store in a California town. He puts a fellow Korean in charge. The earnings support his family. Then he struggles through Johns Hopkins School of Hygiene and Public Health.

It will be interesting through the years to watch that family contributing its insight and experience to both America and the Orient.

The interaction of East and West is anything but one-sided. Several generations ago an American borrowed from a neighbor in Concord some forty books containing the wisdom of India's sages. He also fed his mind on the wisdom of China. From this stimulus working in a Yankee mind came Emerson's famous essay, "The Over-Soul," combining the "Hindu" emphasis on the man-to-God relationship with the "Chinese" concern for the man-to-man relationship.

The neighbor who opened these books from India was Thoreau. He says he mingled the sacred water of the Ganges with the pure water of Walden Pond. But he became famous for the independence of his mind and developed the idea that has had, and is having, a strange influence on the world. The idea is this: If your government is wrong, if for example it sanctions slavery, protest by refusing to pay taxes. This idea he printed in a paper called "Civil Disobedience."

Generations later it fell into the hands of Gandhi whom it definitely encouraged in his passive resistance campaign to free fellow Indians in South Africa who were practically treated like slaves. Gandhi added his own idea: Don't cooperate. At the same time, appeal to your opponent's higher nature in a spirit of good will. It is not the individual you are striking against but the system which really victimizes him and from which you would emancipate him. Our Thoreau contributed to this doctrine, and perhaps also the English Ruskin. So did certain of the Hindu scriptures that proclaim *ahimsa* or non-injury. But the contagion can also be traced to the Sermon on the Mount and a young Jew on a little hill who once faced his enemies with this cry, "Father, forgive them, for they know not what they do." From South Africa the idea leaped through Gandhi's spirit like a spark setting off a forest fire. The British rulers of India felt such fear of his non-violent collective resistance that they dared not let him die in prison. And that power of soul force, that thrust against injustice not with violence but with sacrificial love, has not stopped there. You see it today—changed a little but in essence the same—in the face of Stanley Jones scattering among thousands of American church members this challenge of Christ: resist the military internationale, not with destructive violence but with constructive loving coercion.

Another native of India whose life is a contagion of friendliness is Abraham, Syrian Bishop of Travancore. While studying on this side of the Pacific he went to a Christian conference at Buffalo. At the hotel he asked for a room. "We're full," said the clerk curtly. In his own room in another hotel, Abraham struggled with conflicting emotions: "So this is the way these Americans treat us. I might have been an untouchable!" Then he remembered gratefully the little group of white students who had left the hotel with him in protest against such race discrimination. Slowly the light broke. "This is just the way we treat our outcastes. We Syrian Christians in Travancore never had anything to do with the outcaste people who eat dead meat. Do they feel our constant insult to them as *I* feel this? It's agony. I'd always supposed *they* didn't care." Later that night came the determination: "I'll go back and give my life for those outcastes!"

Eight or nine years ago an American visited Travancore. Abraham reminded him how years before he, as a young missionary, had come to the Indian college and criticized the student and his group for being so smug. There they were, resting back on their oars, claiming that they got their Christianity from the Apostle Thomas who was supposed to have brought the faith direct to Travancore. But judging from the results, their Christianity had been asleep for a thousand years. Weren't they themselves interested only in making money? All that night under the stars the young man had wrestled with his conscience. He did not want to be a parasite. He would do whatever Christ would have him do. He would give his life to save India.

Then came the insult in America and the decision to turn it to good.

And now at length Abraham led the American visitor out to a dry river bed. There on the white clean sand stood a tabernacle consisting mostly of palm leaves. It had cost altogether perhaps $15.00. And thirty thousand Christians were gathered around it. Among them were men who once had been untouchables. But now they were accepted as brothers.

If brotherliness is real, it spreads and nothing can confine it. Not even a prison holding life-term convicts. More than thirty years ago there was an obscure chaplain working in a Japanese jail. He had caught something of the Great Galilean's vision from a missionary who had crossed the Pacific to share it. This chaplain used to pray for the warden that he, too, could see what he saw. The chaplain was removed to another jail. But he kept up the contact. Nearly every day he would write to his former chief. The warden, Mr. Arima, was something of a scholar. It seemed to him that Shintoism, Confucianism and Buddhism were sufficient for Japan and he wrote back excellent arguments. The chaplain's theories failed to interest Mr. Arima, but at last the spirit of the man, his utter dedication to the power of love and his willingness to pay the price for it, convinced the warden. He threw himself into the Christian venture of trust. Gradually the inmates of the prison sensed that he really did see them as children of God.

He became a great administrator in the Kosuge prison of Tokyo. The men were encouraged to do interesting, worthwhile work. There was a choice of something like fifty different trades. In the bakeshop and blacksmith shop, the weaving and dyeing mills, the farm, baseball field and library within the enclosure, they were given the sense of paying their way and not being parasites or robots of the state. They were well fed. One observed little sullenness on their faces.

A Canadian social worker in Tokyo, the late Miss Caroline Macdonald, who used to pray with those about to be executed, once took me to visit Mr. Arima in his office. She pointed out a sheaf of letters a foot high written to the grizzled warden a few months before when he had nearly died from an illness. The letters were from former convicts whom he had helped to find jobs and most of all helped to find self-respect. Before a man was released the warden would often visit the head men of the village where employment was arranged, and through them persuade the people to give the fellow another chance.

Once in a while an inmate would break faith. When the police brought back escaped convicts, Mr. Arima would, in certain cases, greet them warmly, perhaps give them a new kimono and set before them the best meal they had had for days. They had been disloyal to the morale of the place. But they would be treated once more like cooperating members of the group. Some of these returned convicts were so deeply moved by the warden's surprising treatment of them that they underwent a permanent change of spirit.

My guide showed me some unrepaired places in the wall beside the railroad track. Mr. Arima didn't seem to mind. Then she explained.

In 1923 when the earthquake took Tokyo in its grip, the way a terrier shakes a rat, the prison buildings were convulsed, some were smashed to pieces. Mr. Arima, uninterested in his own safety, went about opening up the cells. Everything was in wild confusion. There was nothing to prevent the men from running away. But they rallied round him.

In time a detachment of soldiers frantically approached the warden.

"We hear that a hundred of these prisoners are loose in Tokyo. We insist on setting up a guard to see that no more escape."

"No, I resign first. All my life I have treated these men like friends, and now I won't go back on them, nor will they go back on me."

"But the walls! Your walls are all broken down."

"Yes, but the only way to guard these men is to trust them!"

The soldiers were dubious. "All right," answered Mr. Arima. "Let's take the roll call and see!"

His "trusties" summoned the men; he went through the list. Practically every one of the thirteen hundred, excepting those who were too seriously injured by falling bricks to be on hand, when his name was called, answered, "Here!"

In Kobe, Japan, is a Mrs. Nobu Jo who has been the means of rescuing nearly three thousand women, some so bitterly discouraged about their marriages that they have contemplated suicide. An American magazine suggests that Mrs. Jo should be called a "Japanese missionary to America." Partly from the inspiration of her work in Japan, a similar work has been established in Springfield, Massachusetts. It is claimed that other social workers over here have been vitally influenced by her spirit.

Perhaps the most famous missionary from the East to the West is the half-blind social worker, labor leader, preacher, cartoonist, poet and author of sixty-odd books, a religious genius whom all Christendom is learning to honor. If you want a thrilling biography, try *Kagawa* by William Axling. Read such translated meditations as these:

I am fond of men. The worst, most fear-inspiring, demonized murderer somewhere in his make-up has that which is irresistible. . . .

God dwells in the lowliest of men. He sits on the dust-heap among the prison convicts. With the juvenile delinquents He stands at the door, begging bread. . . . He stands in line with the unemployed in front of the free employment bureaus . . . He who forgets the unemployed forgets God. . . .

Redemption means that when a person has committed a crime against me, instead of revenging myself upon him, I will try to redeem him and give energy for him and put him above myself.

Kagawa, as possibly no other Christian, has the right to say that. For fifteen years he lived obscurely in poverty in the slums. He cannot see out of one eye because he once shared his bed with a homeless beggar who infected him with trachoma. He whimsically accounts for his poor English pronunciation: "Because I refused to give him money for liquor, one of my guests in the slums knocked out four of my front teeth." For weeks he went without lunch so that he could share his diluted rice gruel with the outcastes whom he made welcome in his tiny matchbox of a home. His neighbors were thieves, prostitutes, murderers, imbeciles of all ages. Smallpox, dysentery, cholera and bubonic plague used to scourge the narrow, filthy alley where Kagawa lived. In his six-by-nine-foot room he would take care of the hopeless abandoned cases of intestinal tuberculosis whom he would look for in the street. The odor from their diseased bodies you and I probably could not endure within ten yards. Certainly we would not sleep beside one of them.

During the big strike of 1921, something like eighteen thousand laborers set out to destroy the machinery of the Kagawaki dockyard. He was their strike adviser and it seemed to him foolish for the workers to commit violence and bring down on themselves violence and the ill will of the nation. He saw them advancing in mass formation on a bridge. He stood at the foot of the bridge and prayed with his eyes open, looking straight into their faces. Up from those men went a shout, "Look at Kagawa!" They realized what he wanted and they turned away from the dockyards. The authorities threw him into prison. He was glad of the opportunity: "I was happy because I could meditate with my God and with my Christ."

What set Kagawa on fire? The Gospels! But the American missionary who was unafraid to sleep under the same mosquito net with a Japanese lad suffering from fever, had much to do with touching off Kagawa's enthusiasms and loyalties. And it was the story of an Englishman, forgetting comfort and going down to live among the poor of London, that suggested to the Japanese his astounding venture of love in the slums.

And now his social passion is being reflected across

the Pacific again. A few months ago I visited in Chicago a young couple I had married. Once they had motored a long distance from college to attend a six o'clock morning prayer group of the friends of Kagawa. Now they were graduate theological students, living in a squalid neighborhood that had the reputation of producing more young gangsters than any other section of the city. Their tiny flat cost them twelve dollars a month. There was no rug on the floor. The breakfast consisted of coffee with skimmed milk, an apple, and toast buttered with margarine. The street-car trip to the university consumed an hour and a half a day. Their idea was to build friendships, start interesting activities and thus prevent some of the neighborhood boys and girls who are constantly exposed to the gunplay of toughs from drifting into gangsterdom.

And this young couple was planning to stay there for several years. They were apologetic. "We have it soft compared with our friend Kagawa. It makes us a little ashamed to live so comfortably." What had flashed from Palestine into a Japanese imagination was now kindling the spirits of two young adventurers in the heart of America. And thus, in hidden ways, the leavening process is carried on.

We like to talk about "the East" and "the West," about "China" or "India" or "Japan." These words, in a sense, are but glittering abstractions; there are only human beings living there, or trying to live.

When in 1931 many young Chinese were red-hot in their anger against Japanese victims of militarism who were shelling Shanghai and shooting down Chinese citizens, a Japanese who deeply loved his country sent over to "the enemy land" a delegation of young Christians. They spoke face to face with a group of Chinese, confessing the collective guilt of their people and pledging themselves to do what was in their power to establish justice and peace in the Far East. They represented the conscience which the secretary of Kagawa's peace movement voiced in a Japanese poem of protest:

> We pacifists are still weak,
> We are fighting militarism and imperialism;
> Some day, casting these aside,
> We shall heartily grasp your hands.

In answer, Dr. C. Y. Cheng, then Secretary of the National Christian Council of China, sent a message to Christians of the East and West in Japan, urging them, no matter how strained the relationship between the two countries, to

continue to love each other and remember each other's work in our time of quietness before him who is love itself . . . There is one way to save Japan from her outburst of antiquated Messianism: it is the way of Christian education, the way of enlightened missions. Personal experience of God, a coming face to face with reality in every field of knowledge: here is the essence of what Christian missionaries are offering to Japan and the Orient.

That same spirit is the reason for Brent House near the University of Chicago. Before its hospitable fireplace, little groups of eager American and Oriental students meet under Christian auspices. There are the usual conferences with the experts on international and economic questions. But, most of all, there is an atmosphere of personal intimacy and a chance to enjoy the deeper relationships which all young people crave. Through the mediating friendliness of "Mother" Biller, the ardent nationalist from Korea is able to talk things out with the fellow from Tokyo who was taught to believe that Koreans have no right to independence, and the Filipino can ask embarrassing questions of the American hundred per center.

Granting the urgency of replacing economic and political imperialism with cooperation, such personal intimacy is the most significant contribution which we can make to the Orient and which the Orient can make to us.

In this same city of Chicago a Filipino confided to me that for two or three years he was going around in a circle of despair and bitterness. Nobody appeared to care. The churches seemed to him so many fortresses of race prejudice with moats around them of ignorance. One day an American took him into his home and through his confidence inspired self-confidence. Eventually the two of them worked out a scheme for making other Filipinos feel at home in the city; and now there is a Filipino center supported by various churches, where there is a normal social life and sincere companionship in worship services. From this center, Filipinos go to neighboring churches expecting to be accepted as fellow Christians.

In Los Angeles is another Christian Filipino fellowship, attended also by Americans. An interested pastor of a large church sees to it that they are made to feel at home among his congregation. Inspired by such association, outstanding Christian Filipinos have gone back to the Islands to express not a grievance but good will. One of these has recently been installed as a pastor of the church in the mountain community where Americans and Filipinos spend their summers. He is doing what other guests of ours may soon be doing, if we only grasp the opportunity and share ourselves with these ambassadors to the Far East, ambassadors not of governments but of the future.

You who would spread understanding should strive to release intelligent good will, that solvent of human problems the world over.

CHAPTER SIX

CLIMATE CHANGERS

MARK TWAIN complained that we talk a lot
about the weather but do nothing about it. Each
of us can do something about the climate. ("The climate," he reminds us, "lasts a long time; the weather,
only a few days.") Each of us can help to do something
about the arid atmosphere with which we surround
Orientals in our midst, and dig the irrigation canals
through which understanding can flow to create and
sustain the oases of friendship.

Let us now summarize some of the factors that
make up the old climate and some of the techniques
for creating a new one.

In the United States—including Hawaii—are more
than four hundred Christian agencies at work with this
purpose: to generate a more healthful atmosphere of
comradeship, reverence, faith and renewal for the
Orientals among us.

From the beetfields of Utah, a plodding father comes
to the Salt Lake Union Church. After a week of stoop-
ing and gazing vaguely hour after hour at the soil, it

means something to stand erect with fellow-toilers and join in the Doxology, his eyes shining with "the star of an unconquerable praise."

A brilliant graduate student from Nanking leaves the stimulating cultural atmosphere of a university campus for Dr. Mabel Lee's Chinese Baptist Center in New York City. She can try out some of these new methods of character training in the church school. Most of all in the experience of prayer with Christian friends she can catch a sense of power for good that is more than a theory and more than human.

If you knew Jack Pak (that is not his real name) and how he is involved in home missions, you would sense the value of our Oriental work in this country. A college freshman of Chinese ancestry, he was saving up enough money to pay his way through school.

At the supper table one night Jack heard his father tell about three children huddled in a basement in San Francisco who were next day to be shipped to China. They had just become orphans. Their parents had died in Nicaragua and friends of the family were sending them back to their grandmother in China who was desperately poor and quite unable to take care of them.

You and I, learning of such a pathetic situation, would probably have said, "How pitiful! How sad!" and let it go at that. Not Jack. He ferried across the bay to Chinatown, bundled the three orphans into his

Ford, and took them to his friend, Miss Donaldina Cameron, who knew what to do in such cases. The Commissioner of Immigration was finally located and permission was granted to keep the orphans in their custody for a time. But what to do next? Jack was an ambitious chap, and to him college was a door opening up all sorts of personal opportunities. He had saved up and borrowed more than a thousand dollars to see his way through. But here were the eight- and six-year-old orphan boys on his hands with their frail little two-year-old sister. Was he willing to have them dumped on China with nobody but an illiterate and destitute grandmother to look after them?

He took the two brothers to a home in Berkeley and contributed for their maintenance out of what he had saved for college. This home, named Chung Mei (China-America) had been established by a returned missionary from China, Charles R. Shepherd, and is the only institution of that kind in the country. There are more than fifty boys there. They eat Chinese food and play ball on the American school teams of the neighborhood. During the summer they work together on a ranch in the hills, cutting down wood and then delivering it by truck to customers in Berkeley. The truck they have paid for by presenting programs at conventions and churches, and already they have deposited in the bank a large sum of money towards the new building five miles away. Jack used to get a thrill when he saw his two former protégés marching in the famous Chung Mei band at various conferences and fairs. At present, after getting a fine start here, they are doing well in a South China school. Jack himself has gone ahead in spite of his "vested interest" in the two boys. Eventually he studied at Harvard, and now he holds a teaching fellowship at Stanford University. He and his American wife (one of the rare cases of intermarriage) are planning to put their lives into educational work in China, and hope to adopt the sister of the two boys. Before being finally deported to China this young sister had eight happy years at the Ming Quong Home, which means "Radiant Light."

The personality behind that home for neglected Chinese girls and the service done there is one of the romances of the far West, and is recorded in *Chinatown Quest,* by Carol Green Wilson.[1] Many years ago Miss Donaldina Cameron, enjoying a fine family background and pleasant social opportunities, found what was happening to the little slave girls who were being ruthlessly smuggled through the Golden Gate. Carefully she studied the situation, and soon was conducting a home that was to become famous as "Nine-Twenty," which was its street number. She tactfully

[1] Stanford University Press, Stanford University, Cal. 1931.

refuses to let anyone speak of it as a "rescue home." The name of Lo Mo (Chief Mother), by which she came to be known in Chinatown, is one that is greatly loved and feared. From that friendly red brick house on the hill, which has given refuge to more than two thousand real and potential slave girls, the highbinder tongs could only take pretty "Golden Lily" or young "Peach Blossom" back to their underworld of opium, gambling, prostitution and blackmail, over Miss Cameron's dead body. Incidentally, insurance companies wouldn't take a chance on the lady with the Scots conscience and serene smile who feared God only.

One of the alumnæ of this storm center of Chinatown had an inspiration. The environment was too exciting for the little girls. There ought to be a home for them in a place far removed from the tragedies and conflicts and desperate triumphs of "Nine-Twenty." This Chinese girl dedicated her life to the idea. Today, because of her persistence and the cooperation of Miss Cameron and the home mission forces backing up her work, there stands in Oakland an attractive house, close to Mills College, where about forty girls of Chinese ancestry are being trained to take their part in American or Chinese life. About a hundred young women have gone from Ming Quong or "Radiant Light" across the Pacific to build Christian homes in the new Republic. The first Chinese-trained kindergartner to start work in China got her impetus in Ming Quong.

Then there is that church week-day school, Hip Wo, in San Francisco's Chinatown, where Congregationalists, Methodists and Presbyterians cooperate to equip young Chinese with the Chinese language and culture, so that when they go to China for their careers, as some of them plan to do, they will be more completely at home. In 1932 more than two hundred and fifty pupils attended this school. Many of the subscribers to the work are first-generation Orientals. The place of meeting is the Chinese Presbyterian Church founded four years after gold was discovered in California.

Such Christian enterprises and fellowships as these not only give courage and hope to Orientals who otherwise might become cynical. They create a new atmosphere for all of us in which exploitation and prejudice shrivel up and justice and understanding grow. They change the climate.

"If," declared the Duke of Argyll, "alongside any false or corrupt belief, or any vicious or cruel system, we place *one incompatible idea*—then without any noise of controversy, or clash of battle, those beliefs and customs will wane and die."

Whether engaged in voluntary teaching or full-time service, our home missionaries represent an idea incompatible with exclusion laws and anti-Asiatic feeling. In the light of that idea once embodied in a Workman of Nazareth, the exhausted Hindu melon picker in the Imperial Valley is no longer a mere commodity to be bought and sold on the labor market. The worried Korean widow on her knees eight hours a day in the pineapple fields of Hawaii so that her children can have bread, takes on a strange value. The underpaid Japanese down in the coal mines of Wyoming gets on our conscience. The puzzled Filipino elevator boy in Brooklyn makes us wonder. The inarticulate Chinese laundryman in Vancouver becomes an interesting, significant person.

There is in this country all too little of what Jane Addams calls "social compunction." But suppose this Christian reverence for personality, for which the four hundred and more home-mission centers stand, were eliminated from the American scene and the situation were left to careless, predatory economic forces. Suppose there were no place for East and West to meet on the highest level, no Christian workers going in and out among the Orientals and ourselves, interpreting each to the other, reinforcing our mutual faith. It would be a pretty bleak situation. No, we are not willing to let "the one incompatible idea" lose by default.

What, then, can we do to promote it?

We can more definitely apply our sense of the divine spark in everyone to the Oriental's economic situation. He has converted wild barley fields into carefully-tended farms bearing potatoes and onions; he has painstakingly cultivated the berries, celery, cotton, rice and cantaloups we enjoy on our tables. At least we can be more aware of what we owe to these Orientals. And if the Koreans of the San Joaquin Valley are losing their homes and are unable to find employment in the vineyards and peach orchards we can at least be more sensitive to their need. "I do not ask the wounded person how he feels," cried Walt Whitman while nursing in the Civil War hospitals, "I myself *become* the wounded person."

But sympathy is not enough. We of the church are sometimes called upon to organize a pressure that is non-violent but at the same time unflinching, if the Oriental worker is to live anything like an abundant life. In the Imperial Valley of Southern California, the growers have been hard hit by the depression. One can understand the frantic desire to keep wages down. But one should also recognize what this means to the vegetable field workers, a number of whom are Filipinos. According to an investigating commission appointed by the National Labor Board in Washington,[1] some of these workers have been getting a wage as low as

[1] Report of Feb. 11, 1934, Release No. 3325.

twelve and a half cents an hour and fifty-six cents a day. What they were able to earn was "never sufficient to satisfy even the most primitive needs." The water available on the field was not always fit to drink. To secure less intolerable living conditions, many of these workers, who pick the lettuce and peas we buy so cheaply, went on strike. Here is another example of what underprivileged labor must face.

In January, Rev. Beverley Oaten, a director of religious education, advised a mass meeting of striking lettuce pickers to refrain from violence; late that night he looked into the barrels of twenty-seven revolvers. One of the threatening mob of vigilantes was drunk. He amused himself by poking his cocked weapon into the minister's stomach and then running the muzzle up and down. The click of the steel against the vest buttons seemed to fascinate him. Since then, others (one of them an elderly minister) investigating Imperial Valley labor conditions and violations of constitutional rights, have had to seek protection from mobs in local jails. Low wages, poor living conditions, for any workers within our borders cannot fail to affect the lives of other wage earners. Filipinos and Mexicans in this country have the right to bargain collectively so they can have the chance to live as human beings and not as peons. If white Americans have become victims of war psychology and oppose this right, should not the Christian conscience function in the situation as a sane and vital force?

If you live in a good-sized city, especially in the West, there is probably an Oriental community somewhere about. Invite your home missionary among Orientals to scout around with you to see what conditions are like. Perhaps you will find a dangerously ramshackle building which ought to have been condemned long ago. The landlord, in spite of the depression, is getting heavy interest on his investment. That is because he has been bright enough—probably in violation of the law—to divide up the building into ridiculously small tenements which he farms out to Chinese or Japanese at a scandalously high rate.

There may be sweat-shop labor around the corner. Take the trouble to go down into one of those long basement rooms where Chinese stitch shirts in a stuffy gloom that would sicken most of us. Watch the small boys outside pottering around the cheap gambling places, and ask yourself why no one has cared enough about these youngsters to organize a playground. Don't come back saying to yourself: "That's pretty awful, but I don't see what I can do about it." There is no end to the pressure you can exert if you are willing to go to bat on the issue. Ask your friends to help you stir up public opinion against fire-trap buildings. Organize a committee to bring the matter before the housing bureau. Find out where such shirts are sold. Get facts about the state laws governing the sanitary conditions of labor. Have your church group back up your home mission worker in agitating for a playground for those boys. You can't leave all the pioneering work to one missionary already overburdened. Perhaps it's one of the jobs of your generation to build up a social conscience about such minority groups. The rest of us have sat back and complacently delegated the whole job to someone else.

After all, your church contributes to foreign missions. Your church believes in the lifting up of life. By taking this missionary spirit into the dark alleys where people are being neglected or exploited, you will be making a real contribution. Over at the state university a student is soon to return to China. He has been playing with the notion that religion is an opiate. When he sees young lay Christians doing something concrete to improve the lot of his people, he may be inspired to take back to his country a convincing story of the Christ of the American Road.

To throw a spotlight on society's festering sores, using a scientific approach to facts and a friendly approach to people, is to do the reconciling thing. When the feeling against Filipinos was rising to fever point a few years ago, Dr. E. W. Blakeman, one of the student pastors at the University of California, took an

automobile load of Epworth Leaguers and other undergraduates to Watsonville, where Filipinos had been
molested, and together they interviewed workers and
employers, church people and potential members of
mobs, getting points of view on both sides, and perhaps unconsciously sharing something of their own
Christian sanity with those who had taken leave of
theirs.

Anyone who can make facts about possible jobs
available to young Americans of Oriental parentage
will also render a distinct service. Vocational guidance
is a crying need of second-generation Japanese and Chinese. Church groups or individual members in some
cases might canvass the situation and find an opening or create a spirit that would help an Oriental to
fit in. A young Chinese-American citizen makes this
appeal: "High school and college students and young
people in business can do much in helping the Oriental to get a job by simply understanding him. In that
way the Oriental will become free of the handicap of
unfair prejudice. Give him a job if his ability justifies
it. Be willing to work on equal terms with him. In the
classroom you hardly ever show race prejudice. Why,
then, should you show it in the shop or office?" A
California layman arranged with the company in
which he was an official to try out a young Chinese in
the drafting room. Within a few days all noticeable

prejudice against the newcomer was broken down.

When the Japanese militarists were invading Shanghai there was agitation on the West Coast to boycott the Japanese vegetable men. At various meetings during this crisis the following questions were put to at least one congregation: "If these Japanese who are selling us tomatoes and lettuce and green beans have no connection with the militarists now in the saddle in Tokyo, why should we snipe at them? We may be aiming at militarism when we refuse to buy from them, but is it militarism we shall be hitting? Isn't it only hard-working, innocent folk, some of whom are American citizens?"

Just as in the World War we forgot that our enemy was not the fellow in the opposing trench but the war system, so today in the economic struggle we need to know that the trouble is not that chap who has a job when I'm left out in the cold; the trouble is "the system" which asphyxiates a few individuals with too much money and stifles others with too little.

Once it is recognized that the other fellow is not an enemy or competitor but a fellow runner in a relay race, you naturally desire for him the very best conditions. It won't benefit you if he is made to stumble. It will only delay his passing on the torch to you. Race prejudice is simply an unnecessary obstacle in his path. And if that obstacle is not removed it is our shame.

After many experiences in East and West, Pearl Buck believes that nothing is quite so stupid, so wicked, as pride of mere race. Let us listen to the story that brought home this fact most vividly to this gifted writer:

For years I have made it my habit, a sort of consolation to myself [for the cruelty and evil white people have imposed upon those of other races] to interfere boldly whenever I see anywhere one human being oppressing another. I will not pass by. I stop, however futile it may be, and correct, so far as I am able, that particular incident. One day I saw in Shanghai an American marine give his rickshaw puller a brutal kick. The rickshaw puller in Shanghai is proverbially the poorest and most downtrodden of creatures. He drifts there in extremest poverty from all over China. This one was no exception. He was a middle-aged man and starving thin, and he had been pulling a big American half again his size.

I stopped and spoke to the American with indignation, and the Chinese puller watched this, perfectly understanding what was going on, although I spoke in English. At last he smiled and said to comfort me, "Never mind, lady; look at him! You and I see he is a man of no understanding. Even among white men, if there is one of understanding he does not behave like this."

The rickshaw man was completely superior and he taught me this, that pride of race is always strongest in

those who have the least cause to be proud of themselves.[1]

But pride of race is at bottom sheer ignorance, inad-
equate information, lack of experience. The same author describes the disgust of a Chinese boy, Wang
Ching, when he first encountered a member of the pink
or so-called white race. His father had warned him that
a new family had just come to live inside the city wall,
"very tall and coarse-looking, with the strangest light-
colored eyes and big noses sticking up out of their
faces. The man I saw had red hair, all twisted like
lamb's wool, not proper and straight and black like
ours." One day Wang saw a crowd of his school fellows staring and pushing in a circle about a strange
object. Wang ran up and standing on tip-toe peered between the heads in front of him, until he saw a kind
of boy that he had never seen before.

He was a white boy, dressed in the strangest clothes,
short stockings that left his knees bare, baggy trousers, and
a funny chopped-off coat, and around his neck a piece of
white cloth held by a colored string made of cloth. He
wore no hat, and his hair was almost white, like an old,
old man's, and his eyes were as blue as the long, blue cotton
gowns that Wang Ching wore. His skin was white and
covered with little brown spots all over the nose, a nose that

[1] Pearl S. Buck, "Race Relations and Race Pride," in *Opportunity:
Journal of Negro Life*, Jan., 1933.

was certainly much too big and not like any that Wang Ching had ever seen before.

At first they just stared, but then some of the older boys began to talk. "Did you ever see such a nose? Look at those brown spots!", said one boy. And another said: "No wonder they are called foreign devils. They are worse to look at than the devils in the pictures of hell in the temple!"

We smile at ignorance like that. And yet every day we hear generalizations about other races just as witless. One thing most of us can do to stretch the mind and widen horizons is to become intimately acquainted with some Filipino or Hindu, some Japanese or Chinese. But use discrimination. That is the plea of a young Chinese whose insight applies to other races equally well. "In the choice of Chinese friends, use the same judgment you would follow in choosing a friend of your own race. Keep in mind that not all Chinese are absolutely honest nor are all Chinese cooks and laundrymen."

Dr. Frank Laubach, writing from the Philippine Islands, says that although many young Filipinos over here become extremely bitter towards white people, there is a kindly aspect of the picture; church people do frequently befriend these lonely Filipinos.

I have known a number of Filipinos whose whole attitude towards Americans changed after they had enjoyed week-ends in some church . . . I remember Mayor Phillips of Montclair invited four or five young men to come to his home over Saturday night. When they returned to Brooklyn, I heard them going over and over the experience. I was ashamed to realize how rare such hospitality had been for them. To the end of their lives they will be talking about it. One of the finest contributions that the churches could make in America would be to give the Oriental people such an experience of genuine hospitality. It would not require much trouble and it would be immensely worth while.

In 1932, it is reported, more than eight hundred churches of the Northern Baptist Convention responded to the opportunity to teach English to Orientals, or in other ways show friendliness. As a result at least eight thousand foreign homes were reached and thousands of younger and older Americans benefited from the intimate contact. For most of us, however, the possibilities of inviting second-generation Japanese or third-generation Chinese into our young people's meetings and treating them as we would anyone who happens in, are still almost unexplored.

In a Western city a senior at college discovered that the Chinese church of another denomination needed helpers in the night school for Chinese boys and girls who wanted to learn English. On Friday nights he would collect a car-ful of young people from his church and unload them at the steps of the Chinese church. The residents of Chinatown probably knew no more English grammar after that experience than before. But the young Americans got a different conception of Chinese life from that presented in "Shanghai Express."

Besides supporting agencies which bring Orientals and Americans together in Christian fellowship, and coming to know Orientals within homes, you can inoculate your neighbor with facts. Next time you hear him omnisciently proclaiming that the Japanese have too large families, ask him if he thinks the Takahashi family in Berkeley is a mistake. Then call the roster:

The father is a custom tailor. The mother is prominent in the activities of the Parent-Teacher Association. Both are members of the Quaker church. Elizabeth, a graduate of Whittier College and the Pacific School of Religion, is now a director of religious education. The other ten children have either been graduated from the University of California or presumably will be. Henry is a leader in the Japanese Christian Young People's Conference attended by more than five hundred last summer. He and his brother George are practising optometrists; so is Mary. Another sister is a public health nurse in a Japanese hospital within the state. One brother is receiving recognition as a researcher in zoology at his alma mater. Olive, a junior, is studying commerce; Grace, a sophomore, domestic science. Ernest, a freshman, may become a doctor. The others are in high school. California could do with a few more Takahashis.

Again, if you find your next door neighbor growing dyspeptic over what the Japanese will do when the Filipinos get their independence or what the Mikado's men are plotting on our Pacific Coast now, see if you can't persuade him to feed his mind on a more intelligent newspaper. An unbiased churchwoman out West began the other day to read one of our more lurid morning papers as an experiment. At the end of the week this was her reaction: "If I kept reading those headlines on the first and second page any longer, why, every Japanese gardener and grocery man would become in my imagination a spy." To be a hypodermic educator regarding Orientals you have to read unhysterical books and articles—Dr. Franz Boas and *The World Tomorrow* and Professor Emory Bogardus, perhaps, rather than *True Revelations* and *Sweet Stories of Life and Love.*

Moreover, you will defeat your purpose if you are in too much of a hurry. If the local Y.M.C.A. refuses to allow Orientals in the swimming pool, you can rather successfully stiffen the opposition by denouncing this exhibition of "cultural lag" in a mass meeting of "Hi-Y" boys. Or you can take the trouble to get the ear of the most prominent contributor to the association. To him you can report how a Japanese student Christian leader, traveling one summer in this country, became very angry towards American Christianity because he was not permitted to swim in the Christian pool, whereas, without any embarrassment he was able to go into a city park plunge. If an American, who heard the comment of this young Japanese, had not entertained him in his home and church, he would have taken back to Japan and broadcast there a lurid and eventually exaggerated story that would have undone the life work of three or four missionaries. "Now, Mr. Smith," you might say to the prominent contributor, "the staff at the Y would like to change the ruling against colored people using the plunge, only they believe the constituency would object. If you make it clear that you want the Christian thing done in our swimming pool, you will be strengthening the hand of our missionaries abroad instead of letting their work be cancelled out by our racial intolerance."

There is a political source of irritation to the Japanese, if not to the Chinese and Hindus also, that we can help to remove. It is the Exclusion Act described in Chapter II. Many Christian bodies in season and out have been trying to get this insult removed from the law of the land. You can help by making your senators and congressmen more aware that church people are Exclusion-Act conscious.

Another issue where we can expose minds to the truth is with reference to intermarriage.

One cause of trouble in the social intermingling between Orientals and whites is that we generally wait until the hysteria point is reached, and then we make a direct instead of an indirect attack on the situation. In a Mid-western university a girl resigned from her position as officer in a Christian group because, as chairman of the committee on race relations, she had been pestered, she said, with the attentions of a Filipino. The young man had accompanied her home after a party which she had arranged, and thereafter the telephone bell never stopped ringing until one bright morning her older brother warned her that unless she dropped her committee work and absolutely refused to have a date with that Filipino again, he would beat the fellow up and see to it that his sister had a lot of grief.

But suppose that girl and her family and the Christian organization of which she was an officer had worked out a policy months before. They could have distributed the young man, so to speak, among various families. And it wasn't required of her that she go home with him alone. That older brother might have been educated to the point where he would have invited the Filipino to his fraternity house for dinner and "put him wise." After all, there is such a thing as sublimation, and Oriental students are not incapable of using it. One reason there was so much emotional tension on this particular campus was that one of the many score Filipinos there had gotten into trouble. Anglo-Saxon students had often made the same mistake. But it never occurred to anybody in the community to throw up his hands in holy horror and generalize: "All Anglo-Saxon students are like that. I must never allow an Anglo-Saxon to enter my home or to walk across the campus with my daughter or sister."

Again, there is much climate-changing to be done on the issue of age-prejudice. Maybe Walter Pitkin is right in the title of his book, *Life Begins at Forty*. Anyway, the implications of the following experiment he vouches for should be advertised. One hundred people, varying from twenty-five to eighty-seven years of age, were put through a pretty thorough test. Strange to relate, one fourth of the oldest people in the group showed more accuracy and quickness in their responses than the average! To be sure, the twelve oldest, averaging seventy-nine years, were not up to the general run in agility and skill. But how much slower and less sure in their reactions do you think they were? Just twenty to thirty per cent! Professor E. A. Thorndike tells of a group of young people between twenty and twenty-five years who were set to the task of mastering a new language, Esperanto. They were compared with another group aged thirty-five to fifty-seven. Both did equally well. Youth cannot afford to patronize age.

According to a young Chinese-American who now works in the Chinese Y.M.C.A. of San Francisco, the clash between the two age groups of his race is gradually diminishing. Because education is everywhere increasing, a majority of the parents of his locality can now speak and write English even though recently from China, and this affords them a chance to understand Western ideas and practices. The exposure to fresher ways of thinking will make the parents less insistent, he suggests, on limiting the daughter's activities to the home and the son's marriage choice to their own. In Los Angeles a social worker, eager to have the parents understand the children, conducts in her church a class for Japanese mothers, ostensibly to study English, but really to establish this contact. In that same church other women are beginning to invite Japanese women to their homes. They have been astounded to find that in the city containing the largest Japanese community in America very few Japanese women have ever been asked to sit down under an American roof and knit or chat in a natural person-to-person manner. Friendly, normal, ordinary contacts between Asiatics and Americans are sure to make peepholes through the wall separating the two generations.

In the give-and-take between East and West every Christian can function as a force to reduce kicks and increase good-will. Most of us can do something for world unity by appreciating more profoundly the cultural and spiritual background of the Orientals among us. The younger generation of Japanese and Chinese over here should be encouraged to know and communicate to us more of their Far Eastern skill in art and quietness which would enrich our life in the West. "Native jade can be polished from the stones of other mountains." However, in our eagerness to rub off any provincialism clinging to us we need not be sentimental. The Kingdom of Heaven will not be ushered in by globe-trotters:

"Wot an ugly fice yer 'ave, Bill."

"Oi cawn't 'elp it."

"Well, yer might 'ave stayed at 'ome."

Those of us who stay at home need not wallow in an inferiority complex. We can do some much-needed social engineering right where we are. In Bennington, Vermont, a girls' class saved nickels and at the end of Holy Week forwarded five dollars to the Kingdom of God Movement in Japan. At Christmas time they sent ten dollars more. Christians are in the world, as an unknown writer eighteen hundred years ago expressed it, "to hold the world together." Contributions to missions and to the peace movement do more than we may guess to hold intact the web of life around the globe.

In January, 1934, the Chinese Congregational Church of Los Angeles, cooperating with the Chinese Presbyterian minister, entertained at breakfast some Americans and about thirty Episcopalian, Methodist and other Christian Japanese of both generations. It was not easy for Belgians to break bread with Germans less than three years after the invasion and occupation of Belgium. It is not easy today for Chinese, smarting over Manchuria and the Shanghai incident of 1931, to make Japanese feel at home, even over here. But, around that breakfast table, they succeeded. A Chinese woman, Mrs. J. Kam-Machida, whose husband is Japanese, presided. She introduced her father, an elderly gentleman with the courtesy of Confucius and the most benign of faces. On his head he bears the scar of an early California mob's violence. He did not mention that, but he did recall the founding of the first Christian church for the Japanese on the Coast. It was about fifty-four years ago in the basement of the Methodist church he attended in San Francisco's Chinatown. Mrs. Machida's children, sprung from Japanese-Chinese culture and three generations in a Christian-American environment, may well become a part of the bridge between East and West. It is this international bridge that the new generation is being challenged to build.

Before that cordial meeting in the dining room, another had been held in the church above. For an hour hosts and guests had worshiped together, closing with the Lord's Prayer repeated simultaneously in Chinese, Japanese and English. The service began at six o'clock, the hour when, every Sunday, those California Japanese who are members of Kagawa's Kingdom of God Movement come together to pray. Americans visiting one of their meetings years before had been so stirred by the spirit they found among the professional men, gardeners and farmers (some motoring long distances to be present), that they invited the group to worship in an American church. Out of that interchurch gathering other meetings developed, and now the ice is broken in Chinatown.

While communism fastens itself onto China and the Powers point their weapons at one another, a nervous finger on the trigger, while human beings cry for bread and able men wait in front of employment bureaus, it is no time for any of us to play the dilettante. The issue facing us is critical, urgent, demanding of us every ounce of strength we have. The issue has been stated by Halford Luccock. It is "to evolve a way of living and working together in which belief in a good God shall not be a mockery to millions slipping on the dizzy edge of despair. Our task is to create a moral order of life in our Western world which will make possible the presentation of Christianity to the

Orient as something else than a vast hypocrisy." [1] To be adequate to this task we must first have the climate changed within ourselves.

Political coercion on behalf of Orientals is not sufficient. Multiplied contacts and even compassion are not enough. We must have commitment to God, the passion to enhance life we catch from Jesus.

This commitment brings us sooner or later to a new glimpse of what personality and intercommunication mean: that you and I will appreciate the things we have in common to the degree that we each recognize the other's sacred uniqueness. "Every man," says the young Negro prophet, Howard Thurman, "has something to say to me which will make of my life what it cannot be unless he says it."

In some respects we are all, irrespective of race and color, very much alike on this planet. We all become hungry in very much the same way. We all suffer from the same grief, frustration, pain and fear; we all feel, or would like to feel, the delight of comradeship, the same joy in creating beauty. But in this weird, wild adventure of being alive, each of us occupies a unique point in the universe where he alone can either block God or release the eternal power that makes for life.

Once you get that conception of the terrible sacred-

[1] Halford E. Luccock, *Preaching Values in the Old Testament.* Abingdon Press, New York. 1933.

ness of personality you do not think in terms of Orient
and Occident, of Asiatics and Americans. You think
in terms of men and women, each like a burning glass
focussing or blurring the rays of a sun that is infinitely
greater than any little ego, whether the skin covering
it is black or yellow or white.

You and I will never know the names or more than
guess the appearance of the young Japanese who, or-
dered to go to China and fight, for conscientious reasons disobeyed. It is still a military secret how many
made that stand together as war resisters. An American
over there who should know estimates the number between seventy and a hundred and fifty. We can but
dimly imagine what they said and what exactly happened. Yet, as we think of those trail blazers for a
new Japan and a new world shot down for their con-
victions, we get a reverence for personality beyond all
the irrelevancies of time and nation.

And there are hosts of other persons who are breaking through the camouflage of external things into the
realities of life. One of these is a Chinese woman now
quietly living with her adopted child and her husband
who is a rancher near San Francisco. She used to be
known as Ah-peen (opium) Oie, for she was an efficient drug peddler in Chinatown; and when she would
step into what we now call night clubs, her hair
spangled with the gifts of many men, she was the

recognized toast of the underworld. Slave girls in the red brick home already referred to often had reason to fear her power and greed.

One day a mysterious note was slipped into Miss Cameron's hand asking her to come instantly to the house of this notorious woman slave owner where, the message said, someone was "in great distress." There was a search through the house but no slave girl could be found. Oie was the only person in sight, but surely she did not want to be rescued from her own house! Exactly that. She had written the note herself. She begged for shelter from Miss Cameron. Her life was in danger.

For weeks she was kept in a special room at "Nine-Twenty" under lock and key. A Chinese woman from Canton who happened to be a guest for two weeks at the home used to visit her and chat for long hours every day. Oie caught from that woman a vision of the Christ waiting to be released within herself. She was given a job in the kitchen where she soon became quite expert with the steamed rice and the string beans. The most menial work had a special appeal for her. Girls who had been her slaves she served with her own hands gladly. As a child of fourteen she had been married in China and, while still a youngster, she was sold into slavery in San Francisco. The death of her child, born shortly after her arrival in Chinatown, had embittered and frozen her soul, and in the years that followed she had recklessly gone the way of crime and degradation.

After she had been at "Nine-Twenty" for some time, she heard early one morning what sounded like a kitten outside. Running out she discovered a bundle, such as was often laid on the doorstep of the red brick house, containing a Chinese baby. Oie begged for permission to keep it. By her care of the little boy she proved to the matron's satisfaction that she was capable of the job. In time she accepted a young man who used to plead with her, while she was in the underworld, to leave it all, marry him and come to his ranch. She said yes on this condition—she must be allowed to do the cooking and work in the fields so that she herself could earn money to pay off her debts. From dawn to dark she would toil in the hot valley. The hundred dollars to pay the last debt she brought to town herself. The old merchant to whom she had owed it was surprised; "Why, that was wiped off the books at Chinese New Year seven years ago." But the woman who had once been a power in the opium and slave traffic insisted, "I am a Christian now. I owe the money. You must take it."

That would not have happened unless friends had taken the trouble to know Oie through and through and share with her a life-transforming experience of

God. In our own community there may be an Oriental student preparing for a career in the Far East and waiting for someone to open for him just such inexhaustible resources of life. Or there may be an American of Oriental ancestry hungry for the kind of contact that is found only in small intimate groups where the members trust each other enough to pray together and reinforce the others in their purpose to follow Christ.

When once the electricity of this spirit starts in one person there is no telling how far it will go. Consider this Japanese servant in the home of a friend. The hostess asked me, after coffee was served, to talk about Japan with him in the dining room. He was an ordinary looking man with a face that would betray no romance or adventure. But when he spoke of his life there was light and color. In the homeland he had been a Christian, but during his wanderings and studies in Mexico and in this country he had become interested only in having a good time. A year before he had visited a friend in San Diego who asked him to read three books, *Crossing the Death Line, Love the Law of Life* and *The Religion of Jesus* written by a fellow countryman. When about fifteen years old the author —Toyohiko Kagawa whom we have already met in this book—turned down wealth and chose the adventure of Jesus. A few years later he fell desperately ill with tubercular pneumonia. For a whole morning he read his Bible and prayed. Then he had the feeling of passing over from death into life, of crossing the death line between darkness and light, despair and triumph. The contact with that quality of life blazing out at him from the pages of these books kindled in the mind of that jaded servant a new purpose, to be a channel of the spirit of God. And now every morning he gets up at five o'clock to meditate on the Gospels and to pray. It is his desire to work for others and receive only enough to live. In that way he feels he can render service to God.

The Japanese author, whose writings communicated to a casual houseboy "the glory of the lighted mind," you would not of course take for granted. On the contrary, if he came to your town you would stand in line with hundreds of others eagerly waiting for the door of the auditorium to open so you could see and hear him. Because he is becoming famous as a giant among men, one of the great souls in the world today, you would be expectant, all set. But when I first knew Toyohiko Kagawa I was not expectant, nor all set.

The bow-legged stocky figure, doing graduate work at Princeton, used to hurry across the campus with a load of books under the arm, to the mild amusement of the undergraduates. "That Jap never takes a chance on being late, does he?" And we superior sophisticates would smile patronizingly. We were color-blind. It never occurred to any of us to peer into the life of this man a few years older than we were and get his story. We thought it was more exciting to see the latest screen star. Not one of the pictures we attended had anywhere near the dramatic power and poignancy of the life of that little graduate student in the black suit.

But there we were, rushing blindly off to the movies. No one ever took the trouble to find out how he got along. A professor's wife would ask him to dinner occasionally; then he would fill himself with the food he had looked forward to for many days. At other times he would live on shredded wheat. The dormitory thought the pile of empty cereal boxes in front of his door a great joke.

There will never be another Kagawa. You and I will never have the chance to pass by that particular genius and thus glibly miss an opportunity. And yet the Korean boy, ambitious to help his people win independence, or this Chinese girl training to be a doctor, or that Filipino building up a little prayer group or a Hindu who is just the servant in the house—who knows but that the divine spark in such as these will catch us napping again?

These potential friends, like us, are by no means finished products. But, in a strange way, each one resembles that untouched block of marble in front of which a sculptor once stood, and, before he began his task, paused in wonder to exclaim, "What God-like beauty thou dost hide!"

So Christ stands waiting before us all, whether of East or West.

A SELECTED READING LIST

Groups using *Out of the Far East* as a text for study and discussion will find a fuller list of reference sources on the same subject in *Orientals in American Life,* by Albert W. Palmer, cited below. From denominational literature headquarters leaders may secure a manual by James F. Riggs containing a course on Orientals in the United States, based primarily on *Out of the Far East*. Price, 25 cents. They may also obtain from the same source helpful supplemental material on the theme of this book.

ADAMS, ROMANZO, "Further Developments of Race Contacts in Hawaii." Institute of Pacific Relations, 129 East 52 St., New York. 1933. 15 cents.

"Arms and the Men," reprint of article in *Fortune* magazine for March, 1934. Doubleday, Doran and Co., Garden City, N. Y. 10 cents.

AXLING, WILLIAM, *Kagawa*. Harper and Bros., New York. 1932. $1.00 (after July 1, 1934).

BALLARD, ADELA J., *Roving with the Migrants*. Council of Women for Home Missions and Missionary Education Movement, New York. 1931. 50 cents.

BEACH, WALTER G., *Oriental Crime in California*. Stanford University Press, Stanford University, Cal. 1932. $1.50; paper, $1.00.

BOAS, FRANZ, *Anthropology and Modern Life*. W. W. Norton and Co., New York. 1932. $3.00.

BOGARDUS, EMORY S., *Immigration and Race Attitudes.* D. C. Heath and Co., New York. 1928. $1.80.

BROCKWAY, A. FENNER, *Bloody Traffic.* Victor Gollancz, London. 1933. 3s. 6d.

BROWN, LAWRENCE GUY, *Immigration.* Longmans, Green and Co., New York. 1933. $3.00.

COOLIDGE, MARY ROBERTS, *Chinese Immigration.* Henry Holt and Co., New York. 1909. Out of print; available in libraries.

CRAWFORD, DAVID L., *Can Nations Be Neighbors?* The Stratford Co., Boston. 1932. $1.50.

ENGLEBRECHT, HELMUTH C. and HANIGHEN, FRANK C., *Merchants of Death.* Dodd, Mead and Co., New York. 1934. $2.50.

FELDMAN, H., *Racial Factors in American Industry.* Harper and Bros., New York. 1931. $4.00.

Foreign Student in America, The. Association Press, New York. 1928. $1.75.

GAMBLE, SIDNEY D., *How Chinese Families Live in Peiping.* Funk and Wagnalls Co., New York. 1933. $3.00.

GARTH, THOMAS R., *Race Psychology: A Study of Racial Mental Difference.* McGraw-Hill Book Co., New York. 1931. $2.50.

HUIE KIN, *Reminiscences.* San Yu Press, Peiping, China. 1932.

ICHIHASHI, YAMATO, *Japanese in the United States.* Stanford University Press, Stanford University, Cal. 1932. $4.00.

ISHII, TOKICHI, *A Gentleman in Prison.* Translated by Caroline Macdonald. 1922. Out of print; available in libraries.

KAGAWA, TOYOHIKO, *Christ and Japan.* Friendship Press, New York. 1934. $1.00; paper, 50 cents.

——, *Love, the Law of Life.* John C. Winston Co., Philadelphia. 1929. $2.00.

——, *New Life Through God.* Fleming H. Revell Co., New York. 1931. $1.50.

——, *The Religion of Jesus.* John C. Winston Co., Philadelphia. 1931. $1.25.

KATZ, D., ALLPORT, F. H., and JENNESS, M. B., *Students' Attitudes.* Syracuse University, Syracuse, N. Y. 1931. $3.50.

LASKER, BRUNO, *Filipino Immigration.* Institute of Pacific Relations study. Chicago University Press, Chicago. 1931. $4.00.

LEIPER, HENRY S., *Blind Spots.* Friendship Press, New York. 1929. $1.00; paper, 60 cents.

McKENZIE, R. D., *Oriental Exclusion.* Institute of Pacific Relations, New York. 1928. $1.00.

MATHEWS, BASIL, *The Clash of Color.* Missionary Education Movement, New York. 1924. $1.25; paper, 75 cents.

MEARS, ELIOT GRINNELL, *Resident Orientals on the American Pacific Coast.* Institute of Pacific Relations study. University of Chicago Press, Chicago. 1928. $3.00.

MORSE, HERMANN, ed., *Home Missions Today and Tomorrow.* Home Missions Council, 105 E. 22 St., New York. 1934. $2.00.

NICHOLS, BEVERLEY, *Cry Havoc!* Doubleday, Doran and Co., Garden City, N. Y. 1933. $2.50.

OLDHAM, J. H., *Christianity and the Race Problem.* Association Press, New York. 1924. $1.25.

OSTERHOUT, S. S., *Orientals in Canada.* Department of

Missionary Education, United Church of Canada, Toronto. $1.00; paper, 75 cents.

PALMER, ALBERT W., *Orientals in American Life*. Friendship Press, New York. 1934. $1.00; paper, 60 cents.

PAYNE, PHILIP F., *Gold Mountain*. Friendship Press, New York. 1934. $1.00; paper, 60 cents.

SHEPHERD, CHARLES R., *Lim Yik Choy*. Fleming H. Revell Co., New York. 1932. $1.50.

SPEER, ROBERT E., *Of One Blood*. Council of Women for Home Missions and Missionary Education Movement, New York. 1924. 50 cents.

STRONG, E. K., Jr., *The Second Generation Japanese Problem*. Stanford University Press, Stanford University, Cal. 1934. $1.50.

SUGIMOTO, ETSU I., *A Daughter of the Samurai*. Doubleday, Doran and Co., Garden City, N. Y. 1926. $3.00.

"Unofficial Ambassadors, The," The Committee on Friendly Relations Among Foreign Students, 347 Madison Ave., New York. 1933. Gratis.

WILSON, CAROL GREEN, *Chinatown Quest*. Stanford University Press, Stanford University, Cal. 1931. $1.00.

YOUNG, DONALD R., *American Minority Peoples*. Harper and Bros., New York. 1932. $3.50.

YOUNG, KIMBALL, *The Social Psychology of Oriental-Occidental Prejudices*. Institute of Pacific Relations, New York. 1929. 10 cents.